# VISIONS AND VOYAGES

**To Eric and Pat**

# *Visions and Voyages*

## *The Story of Our*
## *Celtic Heritage*

## *Fay Sampson*

TRIANGLE

First published in Great Britain 1998
Triangle Books
Society for Promoting Christian Knowledge
Holy Trinity Church
Marylebone Road
London NW1 4DU

British Library Cataloguing-in-Publication Data
A catalogue record for this book is available from the British Library.

ISBN: 0–281–05163–1

Typeset by Wilmaset Ltd, Birkenhead, Wirral
Printed in Great Britain by
Biddles Ltd, Guildford and King's Lynn

# Contents

# Acknowledgements

The author and publisher are grateful for permission to use the following translations:

In Chapter 8, 'The cells that freeze', from *Poems and Translations*, Robin Flower, courtesy of The Lilliput Press, Dublin. In Chapter 15: 'The Wish of Manchan of Liath', no. 223, 'St Ide's Wish', no. 226, 'St Columba's Island Hermitage', no. 222, from *A Celtic Miscellany*, Kenneth Hurlestone Jackson, courtesy of Routledge & Kegan Paul, 1951, revised edition Penguin 1971. 'Pangur Ban', from *Poems and Translations*, Robin Flower, courtesy of The Lilliput Press, Dublin.

# A Chronology

*Many dates in this period are uncertain. The following is an approximate guide.*

# *Warning*

The Celts had a love affair with the number three. *The Welsh Triads* are groups of tantalizing cues for ancient stories. Celtic goddesses come threefold, or even three times three. It was an Irish writer who decided there must be three wise men and gave them fanciful names.

So I shall start this book with three warnings.

First: Do not be sentimental about the Celtic saints. They did not spend all their time in woodland clearings, making friends with dangerous animals and writing poetry. The men did not all honour women. Anyone who thinks that Columba was a gentle, humble man is flying in the face of the evidence. Celtic 'saints' were not canonized after their deaths. In this Age of the Saints, the word is used for people who were recognized in their own lifetime by the community who knew them. They might have been proud, hot-tempered, grumpy, prejudiced – but they got on with the work of God. And some actually were humble, generous-minded hermits.

Second: There was no such thing as 'the Celtic Church'. There were many Celtic kingdoms and their churches took different decisions, at different times. Each abbey had its own Rule. Individuals broke the norm. Because something is reported as happening in one place, it does not follow that it was done everywhere. Above all, these local churches did not see themselves as separate from the rest of the universal Church, but as proud guardians of orthodox tradition. They may, however, have been fooling themselves.

Third: We no longer call the centuries which gave us those

brilliant illuminated manuscripts the Dark Ages. Still, there are things we shall never know. Dates are uncertain, scholars differ and revise their opinions, there are conflicting stories. Most importantly, we cannot truly know how these people thought, or why they did what they did. Each of us must weave the available information into our own pattern. The vision that emerges here is my own.

Do we need another book about Celtic Christianity? The shelves are rich with volumes on Celtic spirituality, Celtic prayers, Celtic saints. But the histories tend to divide the material into neat compartments, chapters on individual saints, on Ireland, Wales, Brittany. For me, this misses the exciting reality: that all these people, places, ideas, were strands weaving in and out of each other, like Celtic knotwork. The thread was passing from Britain to Ireland, and back to Scotland and Cornwall, from Wales to Brittany, Ireland to Italy. Irish abbesses were sending their students to Whithorn while Samson and Gildas were at school in Wales. Columba and Kentigern were tackling the Picts from different directions, while Brendan was sailing the islands. Columba was dying on Iona as Augustine was landing in Kent and Columban was upsetting Burgundy. And it was all happening amidst the upheavals of secular history: the Roman empire retreating, Arthur, the Viking longships. It forms a pattern as richly interconnected as a carpet page in the *Book of Kells*.

I have included legends, as well as history, for good reasons. The legends are themselves part of our history. A Britain which did not retell the Arthur story to each generation would not be the same country. A Church which forgot the stories about Brigid and Columba would be the poorer. Even the most fantastic tales can reveal the values of the generation which told them. And hidden among the colourful embroidery there are genuine memories. Without being pedantic, I have tried to indicate this type of material by phrases like 'traditionally', or 'the story goes'.

Personal names come in a bewildering choice of spellings. I have generally preferred the Celtic or English form. But I have made an exception for saints already widely known by another

2

name – thus 'Columba' for Columcille, and 'David' for Dewi. I hope my Celtic readers will forgive me. I have also used 'English', rather than 'Anglo-Saxons'; and 'British' to mean the Celtic people of Great Britain. The term 'Scots' is confusing to modern readers, because the Scots started in Ireland; so I have called them 'Irish' until they are firmly established in Scotland. None of these people called themselves 'Celts'.

# 1
## *Celts*

### *Who were the Celts?*

In the nineteenth century, archaeologists at Hallstatt in Austria uncovered 2000 tombs. Among them, they found the bodies of wealthy chieftains, laid out on four-wheeled wagons. They were accompanied splendidly, with iron swords, twisted bronze collars and other jewellery, helmets decorated with fabulous creatures like the ram-headed serpent, and fine horse trappings. There were enough cooking pots and bones to suggest a sizeable otherworld feast. They had lived around 700 BC. Their discovery opened a window on the Celtic Iron Age.

The Celts are best thought of not as a racial group, but as a range of people with a distinctive culture, speaking a particular group of languages. The Bronze Age society they replaced showed little evidence of warfare, nor high status in buildings and burials. This Celtic Iron Age society appears more aristocratic, with prominent halls for chieftains and prestigious burials.

The culture spread westward. There was another chieftain's burial excavated in Burgundy – a woman in her thirties on a funeral cart. She had a huge bronze wine vessel, nearly two metres high. It was evidence of the status Celtic women could reach. Warriors and rulers were more usually men, but the roles were open to women. Other traces of this show through pagan Celtic stories. The mythical Irish hero Cu Chulainn went to Britain for his warrior training; his teachers were women, Scathach, 'the Shadowy One', and her rival Aife, 'the

4

most famous woman-warrior in the world'. The Welsh hero Peredur got his military training from the nine 'Witches' of Gloucester.

Around 500 BC the heavy wagons in the burial mounds were replaced by light two-wheeled chariots. There was a flowering of distinctive metalwork, enriched with curling and spiralling designs. The skill was better than anything classical Rome could produce.

These people never called themselves 'Celts'. The name *keltoi* is Greek. Romans called them *Galli* – we can trace the echo of that name right across Europe, from Galatia in modern Turkey, through Gaul which is now France, to Galicia in northern Spain, and in the Gaelic language of Ireland, Scotland and the Isle of Man.

They were not a single people, but made up thousands of small chiefdoms, sometimes grouped under a higher king. Their language had different local forms – and so did their gods. They were not given to living in towns, but were a mainly pastoral people, prizing cattle more than crops. They appear heroic, quarrelsome, boastful, heavy drinkers and great meat eaters. They were head-hunters, impaling their war trophies on stakes, even making them into drinking vessels. Cattle-rustling was a national sport. They were reckless in warfare, very good at laments.

The Byzantine Ammianus Marcellinus gives this wonderful description from Roman sources:

> Nearly all the Gauls are tall, fair and red cheeked: terribly stern about the eyes, very quarrelsome, and extremely proud and insolent. A whole troop of foreigners could not stand up to a single Gaul if he called on the help of his wife, who is usually very strong and blue-eyed; especially when she swells her neck, gnashes her teeth, and brandishes her pale arms, which are of enormous size, and starts throwing out punches and aiming kicks, like missiles launched by a catapult.

He did add that they were very clean – even their poor people did not wear rags.

And that is the problem. The pagan Celts were not a literate people. They had a wealth of learning, poetry, history and mythology, but, as a matter of policy, they would not commit their sacred texts to writing. The stories they told about themselves were written down centuries later. The contemporary accounts are what other people said about them. Much comes from the Romans, who came as their conquerors.

They delighted in music and storytelling and the brilliance of language. It would be fair to say that they were cultured, but not civilized. In oral culture, knowledge is most easily memorized as poetry, and the pagan Celts developed a beauty of poetic language. In Ireland, and to a lesser extent in Wales, stories of pagan gods and heroes survived for monks to write them down. These Christian scribes edited the stories in the light of their own scruples, so we shall never know the original versions. But enough shows through to give us some idea of Celtic values, in a way that a Roman eyewitness account cannot do. It is, of course, the higher classes whose stories were told – and even that evidence is difficult to interpret. We can only guess at the history of the common people.

Celtic culture reached Britain around 600 BC. The newer wave, with its brilliant metalwork of bronze mirrors and ornamental shields, followed in about 250 BC. We can trace the westward movement in the languages of the British Isles. The older Goidelic language is reflected in the Gaelic of Ireland and northern Britain, while the later Brythonic group gave rise to Welsh, Cornish and Breton, and probably contributed to the language of the Picts in part of Scotland. But until the Romans came, and for centuries after, there were Celts right across the British Isles.

## Pagan Celtic Gods

The Celts worshipped a multiplicity of local gods, or perhaps a smaller number of gods under local names. A few – such as Epona the 'Divine Horse', who also appears as the 'Great

Queen' Riannon, and Taranis the 'Thunderer' with his wheel – are more widespread. Behind them all was the Mother, single or triple. She was Anu or Danu in the Irish tradition, Don or Modron in the Welsh, or shown as a nameless trio of women. Modron, the Mother, had a Son, Mabon, whose cult was strong in the north of England. In Ireland we find the great Father, the Dagda, a huge club-wielding character with a gargantuan appetite for porridge. His name means 'the Good God' – though this is unrelated to the notion of moral good: he was the god who was 'good for everything'.

The orderly Romans tried to match these gods to their own pantheon. Julius Caesar said that the Gauls particularly honoured Mercury, inventor of the arts. But the problem was that Celts and Romans saw their gods in different ways. The scope of the ideal Celtic god is most clearly depicted in the story of Lugh coming to the court of the gods at Tara. When he demanded entrance, the doorkeeper asked him, 'No one enters Tara without a skill. What do you propose to offer them?' Lugh announced himself as a carpenter, but was told they already had one. 'What about a smith?' 'Goibniu makes our weapons.' 'A warrior?' Post filled. Harper? Poet? Historian? Sorcerer? At the end of a very long list, Lugh laughed, 'Ah, but do you have anyone in there who can do all of these things?' The gods invited him in and made him their leader. He was Lugh Samildanach, the 'Many-Skilled' (in Wales, Llew).

Neither was the ideal human Celt just a battle-hero or poet. He or she was expected to be brave in warfare, eloquent, musical, hospitable, knowledgeable about the arts and law, omnicompetent.

Stories and carvings link the gods with animals. Riannon appears to the hero Pwyll riding a magical horse, quite slowly. Yet Pwyll cannot overtake it however fast he rides, until he hits on the simple courtesy of asking her to wait. 'It would', she remarks drily, 'have been better for your horse if you'd tried that sooner.' When their newborn son is kidnapped, she is accused of infanticide. Her punishment is to carry visitors to the palace like a horse, and her baby is found

7

in a stable where a newborn foal is snatched every year. The Irish hero Cu Chulainn gets his name, 'Chulainn's Hound', when he offers to take the place of a guard-dog he has just killed. He is under a lifelong taboo not to eat the flesh of a dog, and dies when he breaks it. There is the horned god, known in some areas as Cernunnos. A ram-headed serpent frequently accompanies a warlike god. There are ravens, associated with war, swans who may bear golden chains to show they are being held under enchantment, wise salmon, ancient owls, miraculous pigs. Animals do not seem to be worshipped for their own sake, but are closely linked to the gods.

Similarly, goddesses are associated with lands, hills and rivers, but that does not express the whole of what they are. Springs were particularly sacred, especially if a magical hazel tree dropped nuts of wisdom into the pool. All across the Celtic lands, precious metalwork was dropped into sacrificial pools, like Llyn Cerrig Bach on Anglesey. This affinity with animals and sacred wells remained strong in Celtic Christian times.

## Druid Religion

We can recover no theology or religious ethical code. What the gods required was the right performance of ritual for the tribe.

There are reports of four main classes in Celtic society: the aristocrats, from whom chiefs and warriors were drawn; the intelligentsia of druids, bards, seers, lawyers, physicians, artists and skilled craftworkers; a lower class consisting of small farmers, less skilled craftworkers and menial workers; and below them, slaves. It is the druids, the religious leaders, who exercise a powerful hold on the modern imagination – though revivals in the last 200 years owe more to romantic invention than to history. The Romans have left us some accounts, but even those are suspect. One of the most famous descriptions is of a white-robed druid climbing an oak tree by the light of the moon, using a golden sickle to cut mistletoe. Two white bulls are sacrificed and the people feast. In more gruesome sacrifices, human victims are suspended in wicker-work cages and burned. Several reports speak of terrifying blood-stained groves. Even allowing for the tendency of warring sides to spread horror stories about each other, there is evidence of human sacrifice. The Romans themselves had abandoned it not long since and show all the moral outrage of the newly-converted. But the Romans' first encounter with the Celtic population was usually as an army marching in to conquer them. What the Celts did under those extreme circumstances may not have been normal practice.

The Celts placed a high value on cleanliness and personal adornment, but cared less about houses, for themselves or their gods. This characteristic, too, was to show itself in Celtic Christianity. There is scant evidence of temples before Roman times. There are a few enclosures with earth banks and a ditch on the inside, not the arrangement normal in earthly fortifications. These show holes for a substantial pillar and shafts into which ritual offerings were made. A more typical shrine seems to have been a tree or grove – oak, hazel and yew were particularly sacred – and a spring or pool. There might have been a hut of wood, wickerwork or unmortared stone, which housed an image of the god, or some magical object, like a cauldron, weapon, or musical in-strument. On ritual occasions, the priest brought this out to be honoured by the people. Magical cauldrons, vessels of plenty and rebirth, are popular in the stories.

Druids might be men or women. We read of the white robes of the druid with the golden sickle, of a druid in a bull's hide, with a speckled white feather headdress whose wings fluttered. There are descriptions of druid women in black, with gold bands crossed on their chests.

Celts believed passionately in an afterlife. Julius Caesar said the druids taught that souls passed, on death, from one body to another. Some have interpreted this as belief in reincarna-tion. What it almost certainly meant was an assurance of life in the Land of the Ever-Young. There, they would enjoy to the full everything dear to them in their earthly life: fighting, feasting, song. So complete was this faith that their enemies marvelled at how careless of death they were. This joy was not a reward to be earned, but a natural right.

Their stories suggest that the Otherworld was very close to them. At any moment, the chase of a stag, the appearance of a beautiful woman or a repulsive hag could be their invitation to cross the threshold. It could lead to great joy, but it might be dangerous and difficult to return. That boundary with the supernatural was at its most open on the night of Samhain, the start of the Celtic year at the beginning of November. Today, Christian Iona is said to be a 'thin place', where the boundary between the physical and the spiritual is almost non-existent.

Britain was known as the headquarters of druid religion and its intellectual centre when the Romans invaded Britain in force in AD 43. The occupying power had reason to fear the druids, beyond the moral outrage at human sacrifice. Unlike most levels of Celtic society, the learned class was free to travel across tribal boundaries. They were the guardians of Celtic cultural identity. In a country with many quarrelling chieftains, the druids were in a unique position to become a unifying force and a focus of opposition to Rome.

Their headquarters were on the island of Mon, which the English later named Anglesey. The general Suetonius Paulinus attacked in AD 60. The Roman historian Tacitus described the invading army preparing to cross the Menai Straits in a fleet of small boats. On the opposite shore they saw the massed ranks of druids, the women in black gowns, determined to resist them with weapons and magic. The sense of the outraged gods of this island struck terror into the hearts of the Roman soldiers. But their officers rallied them and the assault was launched. As they stormed up the beaches, the soldiers had to fight their way through cursing druids to reach the sacred groves. The priests were howling, raising horrified hands in supplication. Women ran screaming through the chaos, brandishing flaming torches. The Romans destroyed the sanctuaries and killed their guardians. The possibility of the druids uniting Great Britain was destroyed.

Local forms of their religion persisted. Ireland was never

part of the Roman empire. Druidic tradition remained its established religion, gradually modified by contact with a changing Europe.

For those whose vision of Celtic Christianity has been a hermit living a simple life beside a waterfall, singing poems of praise to a blackbird, and eating a vegetarian diet, some of these characteristics of Celtic society may appear startling. Are these really the same people?

The apparent inconsistencies owe more to our sentimental imagination than to the reality of the evidence. Even in the Age of the Saints, we still find stories of hot temper leading to bloodshed, of a near-fanatic disregard for the limitations of the human body, of proud autonomy and diversity that eventually allowed the Celtic churches to be picked off piece-meal by their more disciplined Roman opponent. But in the picture of the hermit we can trace some older elements too: the sacred spring, the animal companions, the eloquent poetry, the inappropriateness of a prestigious building to house the God of the whole earth. The Christian hermit or abbot could be female as well as male, and quite capable of giving a king the rough side of her tongue for his soul's sake. This independence of mind, the love of learning and art, the freedom of the sacred person to travel, are part of the immense attraction of Celtic Christianity.

# 2

# *Romans*

## *Glastonbury*

How and when did Christianity come to Celtic Britain? We should love to know. There is a persistent tradition that the earliest church was in Glastonbury.

One story goes that Joseph of Arimathea had a chalice containing blood from the pierced side of Christ. Joseph gave his own tomb for Christ's burial, and later set sail with twelve companions for Britain. At Glastonbury, on Chalice Hill, they buried the precious vessel. In the Arthurian romances, this has become the Holy Grail, a Christian version of the Celtic magic cauldron, offering eternal life and spiritual plenty. Joseph planted his staff on Wearyall Hill, where it took root and flowered. From that sprang the thorn tree which flowers in mid-winter, and from which sprays of blossom are cut to send to the monarch.

Another legend says that Joseph of Arimathea was Jesus's uncle, and that he brought the Christ-child to Britain on a merchant voyage. That inspired William Blake to write:

> And did those feet in ancient times
> Walk upon England's mountains green?
> And was the holy Lamb of God
> On England's pleasant pastures seen?

Sadly, the answer is almost certainly, no. Stories about the thorn and the chalice did not begin to circulate until hundreds of years later. The earliest evidence for Christian activity at Glastonbury dates from the sixth century.

12

But Christianity did reach Britain early. And it could have been brought by merchants from the Mediterranean. There was a flourishing trade, with British chieftains importing wine, oil and corn. In return, the principal export was tin from the south west, as well as gold, copper, dogs and slaves.

## Roman Invasion

Still, the most likely means by which Christianity reached Britain was the Roman conquest. The soldiers brought their religions with them, official and unofficial.

In the summer of AD 43, a Roman army of 40,000 soldiers massed on the shore at Boulogne, under the command of Aulus Plautius. This imperial force had carried the might of Rome around the Mediterranean and across Europe. Now they had reached the north-west edge of the Continent, the end of their known world. The soldiers viewed the low smudge of Britain across the Channel with trepidation. They had heard rumours that there was an otherworld island out in the west. Fishermen were woken in the dark and compelled to act as ferrymen on a ship carrying the invisible dead. Was this where their officers were taking them? They mutinied. It was an ex-slave, Narcissus, who mounted the rostrum and dared the free-born Romans to have the courage to follow where their standards led.

The army embarked. This time the occupation was permanent. And in the wake of the legions came the camp followers and civil servants. They brought a medley of religions with them.

Official religious cults were observed throughout the Roman empire. The emperor was not worshipped as a god in his lifetime, but veneration was paid to his *genius*, the spirit through which he ruled. Qualities useful to encourage in soldiers became minor deities: Virtue, Victory, Discipline, Fortune. Romans who were far from what they thought of as civilization honoured the touchingly-named Fortuna Redux, the 'Home-Bringer'. The standard of the legion was

13

sacred, almost a god in itself. It had its own shrine, and was taken out to be anointed and garlanded with roses in May. And there was the whole cast of deities from classical mythology, with Jupiter at the head.

Britain had been in contact with the Roman empire for a long time. Kingdoms in south and east Britain accepted Roman occupation. Further west, at Maiden Castle in Dorset, the conquest was bloodier. The Celtic warleader Caradoc, known to the Romans as Caratacus, rallied opposition in what is now Wales. He was defeated at Snowdon and fled for refuge to the northern British kingdom of the Brigantes, but their ruler, Queen Cartimandua, the 'Sleek Pony', handed him over in chains. Caratacus was paraded as a captive in Rome, where his courage and dignity so impressed people that he was then treated honourably. The legions pushed west and north, overcoming the druid stronghold on the island of Mon in AD 60.

Suetonius Paulinus must have thought he had crushed the spirit of the British. But, almost immediately, ghastly news reached him. Prasutagus, chief of the Iceni in East Anglia, had died, leaving half his huge wealth to his two daughters and giving the other half to the megalomaniac emperor Nero. But Catus, the imperial procurator, decided to seize Prasutagus's whole land in brutal plunder. The widowed queen Boudicca was flogged, her daughters raped.

Boudicca raised the standard of vengeance. Invoking her goddess Andraste, 'Victory', she released a sacred hare. Then she led the battle, standing tall in her chariot, spear in hand. The Iceni overran the local Roman garrison. They sacked Colchester, where veterans from the Roman army had been allowed to settle. They rampaged on to the thriving commercial port of London and burned it, slaughtering men, women and children. There are stories of women prisoners taken to a grove and dedicated to Andraste. One horrified Roman said that the captured women's breasts were cut off and stuffed into their mouths before they were impaled on spears. Eventually Roman reinforcements arrived, the shocked legions rallied and took their own vengeance on the rebels.

Yet the worship of Boudicca's goddess was not suppressed. Andraste was assimilated into a Roman–Celtic pantheon. There was an uneasy sense that this was still her land.

## Romano-Celtic Religion

Official cults were often soulless observances. The Roman legions and their foreign auxiliaries brought a host of other gods with them. It was official Roman policy to match these with local gods. Taranis the Thunderer was linked with Jupiter, who also hurled thunderbolts. At Bath, the Celtic goddess Sulis was worshipped at the hot springs. When the Roman built baths there, her name was joined to that of Minerva, the classical goddess of learning revered by doctors. All over the country similar matches were made. But these linked deities never meant quite the same thing to Celt and Roman.

A hybrid Romano-Celtic religion was growing up. Sacrifices were made. If an animal was slaughtered, the organs might be examined by a trained prognosticator. There were libations of wine and offerings of corn. A favourite gift to the gods was a silver plaque shaped like a feather, inscribed with the worshipper's intention. Shrines were decorated with these gifts, and with flowers and ribbons, just as the Celts tied cloth on sacred trees at wells. Precious metal was used for gifts to the gods, base ones for cursing. There have been many finds of lead tablets calling down retribution on a thief. There was a strong business element in Roman religion. It was not unusual to offer the god a fixed percentage of the stolen goods if they were recovered. There are offerings of model arms, eyes, breasts, in metal or ivory, which are the worshipper's plea to the god for healing, or gratitude for a cure. The likelihood is that much of this was not too far from the Celts' dealings with their own gods.

This hybrid religion gave rise to a local style of building-square, with a high central structure letting in light through clerestory windows. Stone, as well as wood, was used, rare in Celtic tradition. One interesting building complex is the temple of Mars Nodens, built at Lydney in Gloucestershire, above the River Severn. Here, Nodens was almost certainly worshipped in his role as a healing god. As well as his temple, there were baths, a large guest house and a long building with cubicles. Devotees probably lay down there and submitted themselves to sacred sleep, with dream-tellers on hand to interpret what they saw.

The Romans divided Britain into two provinces: Britannia Superior, the southern and eastern parts nearer to Rome, and the more distant Britannia Inferior, in the north and west. Away from the centres of Roman activity, religious life probably continued much as before. The druids were not eliminated everywhere. Indeed, some Romans admired them as philosophers and keepers of wisdom. Change was most evident in the cities, the wealthy villas and the military camps.

## Eastern Religions

Other religions came from further east. A rival to the emerging Christianity was the cult of Mithras, a favourite with soldiers. He was a warrior god in the service of the great Ahura Mazda. He slays a bull whose gushing blood brings all life into creation. Against Ahura Mazda fights the demon, Ahiriman, who sends a scorpion to attack the bull's fertility. Only Mithras's valour defends the life of the world. A line of sacred text survives: 'You saved us, after having shed the blood eternal.'

His temple, the Mithraea, was usually partly underground. Here, men were initiated into successive grades of Raven, Bride, Soldier, Lion, Persian, Courier of the Sun, Father. There were terrifying rituals to be undergone. Candidates were symbolically buried alive. There were feasts at which initiates might wear the masks of raven or lion to wait on the higher grades. The cult had a strong link with the sun. In the thick darkness of the temple, light was made to shine from behind Mithras's head, haloing it like the sun's rays.

We can catch echoes of modern freemasonry in Mithraism. It practised secret initiations into successive grades. It was particularly popular with army officers and with wealthy merchants, who could find a welcome from the brotherhood in foreign ports. It was for men only, particularly men of high status.

More appealing to women, as well as men, was the cult of Isis, the religion of the Egyptian goddess whose husband Osiris, or Serapis, was killed by the jealous god Seth. Isis brought the dismembered Serapis back to life, and he became a god of the Otherworld. She is pictured suckling her infant son, Harpokrates, who became a hero warrior. They form a triad of creative power.

Like Mithraism, the worship of Isis had its own secret initiations and knowledge. But it placed little value on violence and blood sacrifice. Celibate priests, wearing white robes, processed carrying jugs of water supposed to be from the Nile, and posies of flowers. Its rites were full of light and singing. The moral code of its adherents made it admired by the more thoughtful.

In contrast was the cult of Cybele, the Great Mother of Asia Minor, Mistress of Beasts, the Mother of the Gods. Her priests castrated themselves to honour the remorse of her unfaithful lover Atys, who died afterwards and rose again.

We have no evidence of Jewish worship in Roman Britain, but it is not unreasonable to suppose that it came with the rest. One of the first British Christian martyrs (whom we shall meet in Chapter 3) bears a Jewish name, Aaron.

And along with all this seething cauldron of beliefs came Christianity. The early Church was anti-militaristic, but there certainly were Christians in the Roman army. Christianity gained a foothold in the British Isles while it was still a minority faith, long before the Emperor Constantine gave it most-favoured status across the whole empire. Why? What had it got to offer to expatriate Romans and native Celts?

It appealed to the heart, in a way the official Roman cults never could. It had a Saviour-Hero. But unlike Mithraism, it was open to everyone, male or female, rich or poor, free or slave. It offered hope. Humans were no longer at the mercy of capricious and unpredictable gods. It introduced a moral

17

dimension lacking in traditional Celtic religion or in most Mediterranean cults. Its vision of heaven took the physical joy of the Celtic Otherworld into a new spiritual dimension.

# 3

## *Martyrs*

### The First British Christians

There are competing claims for the first named Christian in Britain. Two are very early.

Christianity was only ten years old when Aulus Plautius led his legions ashore to invade Britain. The first candidate is his wife. Pomponia Graecina was British. Four years after invading Britain, Aulus Plautius handed over the governorship and took her back to Rome. There, in AD 57, she was accused of 'a foreign superstition'. That could mean that she practised the druid rites of her Celtic ancestors. Yet, despite the raid on the druid stronghold soon after, Celtic religion was never forbidden.

Or it might mean that she was a Christian. Rome was tolerant of most other beliefs. It was uneasy about Judaism, with its one God and the refusal of its adherents to make even formal offerings to Caesar. Still, provided the Jews did not use their religion to foment rebellion, the Roman administration made a special case for them. Christianity, on the other hand, was seen as dangerous. It was spreading fast. It too taught that there was one God, and its followers refused to compromise by making offerings to the emperor's *genius*. That could weaken the loyalty which bound this huge diverse empire together. Real persecution came only later, but soon after Pomponia Graecina's accusation, Paul was executed in Rome, not for his theology, but for endangering the peace of the empire.

A stronger candidate is Sergia Paula, wife of the Roman

commander in York in AD 79. It was the custom for Roman women to take the feminine form of their father's name. We meet a Sergius Paulus, who may have been her father, as pro-consul of Cyprus in Acts 13, when Barnabas and Saul went there on a mission. He was 'a man of understanding', living at Paphos, who was converted after Paul temporarily blinded the local holy man who argued against him. He may not, of course, have been the only Sergius Paulus in the Roman empire.

From first-century army wives, who may or may not have been Christian, we enter near-certainty with Alban. He lived in or near the Roman city of Verulamium, now St Albans. When, is unclear. The eighth-century writer Bede places it around 304, but the evidence points most strongly to the persecutions of the 250s.

A Christian priest, on the run from arrest, arrived at Alban's house, where he evidently expected to be received sympa-thetically. Alban sheltered this asylum-seeker for several days and their conversations led to his conversion. Then pursuit caught up with them. Alban put on the priest's long, hooded cloak and distracted the posse long enough for him to escape. When the soldiers discovered the deception, they dragged Alban before the judge. Threatened with torture, Alban declared that he, too, was a Christian. When the in-censed judge demanded to know his name and family, the prisoner declined to say anything except that his parents had named him Alban and that he was now a follower of the true and living God. This could indicate that he was a local Celt, not one of the Roman establishment. After his refusal to make an offering on the altar, the test of loyalty to the emperor, he was flogged. He still would not recant and was sentenced to be beheaded.

The early tale tells how Alban was led out to the hill of ex-ecution. The bridge was so packed with onlookers that he could not cross, yet he was so intent on martyrdom that he pressed forward and the river dried up to let him pass. At this, the soldier designated as executioner lost his nerve, threw down his sword and begged to die in Alban's place.

Still Alban went on, up the grassy hill through a carpet of spring flowers, to where another executioner was waiting. A spring of water bubbled up for him to drink. Then he knelt and bowed his neck. As soon as the bloody deed was done, the executioner's eyes fell out.

There is no reason to doubt the main facts. Alban's grave quickly became a place of pilgrimage and worship. The story of his martyrdom was known early on the Continent and churches there were dedicated to him.

Two other names surface around this time: Aaron and Julius – who were also tortured and beheaded. Aaron's name suggests he was of Jewish origin. The city of their martyrdom was most likely Caerleon-upon-Usk, showing that Christianity was by then widespread in Britain.

Three martyrs' names in little more than two centuries after the death of Christ. Bede, writing in the eighth century from older records, says there were many others of both sexes, across Britain. Then as now, Christians whose names are known only to heaven paid the supreme penalty for keeping the faith.

## Imperial Favour

Early in the fourth century, there was a momentous change. Christianity, still a minority faith, became the most-favoured religion of the Roman empire.

Constantine was in York in 306 when his father, the Emperor Constantius, died. It was on British soil that Constantine was offered his father's title of Augustus of the Western Empire. He went for it, in the face of opposition. He was not at that time a Christian, but as he was fighting his way to supremacy in Rome, he had a vision. He saw a cross superimposed on the sun with the words, 'In this sign, conquer'. He had his soldiers paint the Greek initials of Jesus Christ, the *chi-rho* monogram, on their shields. They were victorious.

Constantine expressed his gratitude by lifting the penalties then in force against Christians. In 313, he and his brother-in-law, the Eastern Augustus, agreed on the Edict of Milan. There was to be toleration for all religions and full restitution of wrongs done to Christians. Constantine declared the Christian God to be the high divinity and himself his servant. From being a sometimes persecuted minority faith, Christianity was now the favoured religion of the empire. With the exception of one subsequent emperor, it remained so.

Constantine was not baptized until the end of his life. It is hard to say how far he really understood Christianity. He declared Sunday a public holiday. The connection with the sun was as important to him as the fact that it was the Lord's Day. He liked the idea of celebrating Christ's nativity on the mid-winter feast day of the old sun god. He called himself the 'Unconquered Sun', a title used for both Mithras and Christ.

This parallel was not lost on others. Evidence from that time has been uncovered in London. At Walbrook, the Mithraea was wrecked and the statue of Mithras smashed. It is hard not to see this as the act of Christians now in the ascendant. They feared Mithras was too close a rival to Christ.

## The British Church

The Church in Britain had not waited for official approval. Early on, we read of British bishops. When a council was held at Arles in 314, only a year after the Edict of Milan, three bishops represented Britain. That is unlikely to have been the full number of dioceses. The British delegates who attended had sees at London, York, and possibly Lincoln. This fits well with the civil administration of Roman Britain, which had now been divided into four regions. It is probable that a fourth episcopal centre would have been Cirencester. There could easily have been more.

British bishops crop up again in 343 at another council in Sophia, in modern Bulgaria, and they were at Rimini in Italy in 359. On the latter occasion, a slightly disapproving note states that three of them accepted the offer of expenses, which were usually declined. Their excuse was that they were short of funds and did not want to be a burden on their Christian friends. Given the travelling distance from Britain, and the fact that the council lasted for several months, this seems not unreasonable. That need not mean that the British Church was unusually poor. The implication is that there were other British delegates from churches wealthy enough to carry the expense. These dioceses may not have been on the modern scale. As few as 100 worshippers in a city might be enough to warrant a bishop, with priests serving outlying communities.

Christianity spread, taking in serving soldiers, Roman colonialists, other foreigners and native Celts. It almost certainly took root first in Roman bases like Verulamium and Caerleon, 'City of the Legions'. The British Church adopted the pattern of management based on the local government structure of the Roman empire. Words like 'diocese' and 'parish' are taken directly from civil service vocabulary. Respect was given to the bishop of Rome as first among equals, but the idea of a pope having authority over all Christendom had not been established in any country. There is no evidence of anything distinctively Celtic about this early British Church. But the rapid spread of Christianity can be traced in the specialized words, like the *Offeren* or Eucharist, which entered the Celtic language at an early stage.

As the Church grew, buildings had to be converted to Christian worship or specifically constructed. Some were town churches, like the temples and shrines of other faiths. Then there were cemetery churches, which grew up round the tombs of saints or martyrs like Alban. To conventional Romans, who did not allow burials inside the city walls, the idea of worshipping regularly in a cemetery was abhorrent. Still more bizarre was the idea of living alongside the tomb of a martyr, as some Christians began to do. Christians buried their dead in the sure hope of the resurrection, perhaps imminent. To preserve them uncorrupted, corpses were sometimes encased in plaster. One such gypsum burial is of a ten-month-old baby, daughter of a Roman soldier, probably Christian. Simplicia Florentia is recorded as 'a most innocent soul'.

23

A third place of worship was the private house. A room of a Roman-style villa was sometimes set aside, with frescoes or mosaics to indicate its Christian use, or a separate building might be constructed in the grounds. At Lullingstone in Kent there is evidence of a split in the family. Pagan gods were worshipped downstairs, the Christians' God in the room above. One particularly intriguing find is a mosaic pavement from the villa of Hinton St Mary, Dorset, now in the British Museum. Around its sides are themes which could be mythological – the hero Bellerophon riding the winged horse Pegasus and slaying the serpent-tailed monster Chimaera. At the corners are the four winds. But the central face is of young, beardless man with huge dark eyes. His head is haloed by the *chi-rho* monogram, a symbol of Christianity even older than the cross. It is hard not to interpret this as a picture of Christ, possibly the oldest surviving portrayal in the western empire. We could interpret Bellerophon as Saint Michael battling against Satan, the four winds as the evangelists giving breath to the Gospels. Yet what is the face of Christ doing on the floor, where it can be trodden on? Is this evidence of a Christian chapel, or was the villa-owner hedging his or her bets, giving a decorative nod to Christianity to satisfy some family members and friends, while offering pagan myths for those who preferred the old ways?

We have no liturgy from the early British Church. Baptisteries are sunk in the ground, but are not deep enough for immersion, suggesting that water was poured over the candidates. Lead tanks have also been found with Christian symbols, possibly portable baptisteries for scattered congregations. After instruction, catechumens were presented for baptism at Easter or Pentecost, or later, Epiphany. Their worldly clothes were stripped from them, they descended into the water and the priest or bishop, standing above, poured copious quantities of water over their heads in the name of the Trinity. As they rose from the water, they were given a new white linen robe. The baptismal robe was traditionally worn for the next 40 days. Priests, but not deacons, were qualified to perform baptism. But because confirmation followed immediately, it was usually done by, or in the presence of, a bishop. It is impossible to know how strictly these rules were carried out in remote areas, where bishops were thin on the ground. Evidence from Samson's time in the fifth century suggests they were not always followed. When Augustine arrived in Britain at the end of the sixth century, he had a fierce argument with the British Church. One of the issues was baptism.

In the light of later conflicts with the Roman Church, it is important to keep in mind that the Church in Britain was founded early, and on the Roman model – a secular, diocesan Church. Long after the legions left, it continued to think of itself as loyally holding to ancient tradition. Looking back, we may see evidence of change, but the Churches in the British Isles seemed unaware of its implications. Celtic Christianity never thought of itself as a breakaway movement or a reformation.

# 4

## *Independence*

### *The End of Roman Rule*

Within a century of their Church emerging into the sunshine of imperial favour, British Christians found themselves abandoned by Rome and threatened by heathen invasions. Would they, and their newly independent Celtic land, survive at all? And what would it mean now to be the Church in Britain?

At the start of the fifth century, on the northern frontier around the reinforced Hadrian's Wall, Britons and Romans alike were trying to hold back marauding Picts. English longships were beginning to harry the land from the east. Pirates from pagan Ireland came raiding from the west. And at home, Rome had problems of its own.

Colonial empires are not universally popular in the lands they occupy. Urban upper-class Britons and rural landowners had slipped comfortably into the Latin language, Roman lifestyle and Italian-style buildings. Imperial rule fell heaviest upon the rural poor. What Rome wanted from Britain was food, and agriculture paid the heaviest weight of taxes. Landowners, in turn, ensured that the peasants paid the greater share of that burden.

In 409 there was a revolt, which seems to have occurred in the south, particularly the south-west. The peasants rose against their local rulers. They lynched some. They expelled the Roman administrators, abolished the rule of Roman law and declared secession from the Roman empire – the first of all its territories to do so. The effect of the uprising was limited, however. They simply replaced the hated rulers with more sympathetic landowners. They did not take over the estates, as their counterparts in Gaul did later.

A year later, the whole imperial system began to crumble. Angles, Saxons and Jutes were crossing the North Sea in their longships in increasing numbers. They wanted more than plunder from Britain now: they saw an enticing prospect of good farming land for settlement. Meanwhile, Visigoths from the north poured southward across Europe, fleeing the Huns. They crossed the Danube, killed the emperor and, in 410, temporarily captured Rome itself. Those British leaders still loyal after the rebellion sent an urgent appeal to Rome for help. The answer was shattering. They were told that from now on they were on their own.

When Roman troops withdrew, they were not replaced. The military and civil administration which was left behind was no longer paid, and the imperial occupation collapsed, bringing the economy down with it. The old certainties were gone. Out of this momentous period emerged a Briton whose ideas rocked the Church in Europe, Asia and Africa.

## *Pelagius*

Pelagius was born in Britain around 350, of a well-to-do Romano-Celtic family. He arrived in Rome in the early 380s, possibly as a law student. He clearly had a good education, speaking fluent Greek as well as Latin. Pelagius represented the classically educated Christian humanist tradition which increasingly distinguished the British Isles from developments in the Church elsewhere. Soon he was baptized and turned his attention to Christian doctrine. He read widely, especially the Church Fathers. No one wrote a flattering *Life* of him and he gives away very little about himself in his own writings. Our information comes mostly from his opponents. Their picture is of a fat bull of a man who moved 'at the stately pace of a tortoise', and had the build and strength of a wrestler. They mocked his Celtic origins, saying he was 'weighed down with Scottish oats'. Despite this, he was evidently popular. He may have been the 'gossiping monk' Jerome of Bethlehem complained of, and criticized for the number of his women friends and the fact that when they invited him to give them instruction, some of them entertained him in their bedrooms. Yet the purity of Pelagius's lifestyle impressed those who knew him.

Pelagius was not ordained and probably never was a monk, in the sense of taking vows or joining a monastic community. But he did advocate the monastic lifestyle, wanting Christians to live chaste, disciplined lives. Celibacy was the ideal. He did not condemn matrimony, but encouraged couples to abstain from intercourse once their family was complete, and devote their energies instead to prayer and charity. He appears at first to have been more interested in moral reform than theology.

While in Rome, he wrote a commentary on Paul's epistles, which aired his views on grace, free will and baptism. The theology of the Church was still being developed. It had got as far as the question: 'Who is Jesus Christ?' – and had hammered out a doctrine of the incarnation and the Trinity. Attention was about to be focused on the atonement.

The Visigoths attacked Rome in 410. Pelagius and his friends fled across the Mediterranean with thousands of others, and he arrived in Carthage, on the Gulf of Tunis. It was the home of Augustine of Hippo (not the Augustine who later came to Canterbury). Augustine was the same age as Pelagius. Both had energetic minds, keen to pursue the truth as they saw it. Neither of them accepted criticism passively. At first Augustine praised the holiness of Pelagius's life; then he learned more about what he was teaching.

As a young man, Augustine had fallen under the influence of the Manichees, a sect with a vivid doctrine of the world in the grip of dual powers – Good versus Evil. After his conversion to Christianity, he changed to believing that humans have a choice, whether to do wrong or right. Then his views swung back. Through Adam's pride and lust, Augustine taught, evil has so enslaved all humankind that it is impossible to resist. Every human being is trapped in original sin, passed on through the sexual act, and can only be freed by the gift of God's grace. If someone is not saved, that is because God has decided against it. There is nothing anyone can do to achieve their own salvation, if God does not will it.

Pelagius protested. Such a corruption of humanity denies the goodness of the Creator God: 'If we were filled with old sins in our mother's womb, that would make the devil our maker.' He believed that humans are indeed saved by God's grace, freely offered, but that human will is also required. It is our free choice whether to reach out and take hold of that great gift through baptism. His views on infant baptism were fuzzier, since it should have followed that it could not effect salvation, but he never claimed this.

Pelagius was not promoting a revolutionary theology. Rather, he was defending the classically-influenced, humanist Christianity of a more secure age. It was his arch-opponent, Augustine of Hippo, whom he believed was distorting the faith with this new doctrine of original sin and predestination. Is it fanciful to think that the shaking of the empire in Britain made Pelagius passionately aware of our need to assume some responsibility for our own destiny?

The two men and their supporters clashed in fierce controversy. It is largely against Pelagius's views that Augustine wrote his great book *City of God*. Pelagius was a lay scholar. The clerical hierarchy saw the Church as the community of the elect, with themselves having the unique power to mediate the grace of salvation through the sacraments. Implicit in Pelagius's notion of free will, the ability of the individual to turn to God and grasp salvation, was a challenge to the role of the clergy. A council of African bishops met and condemned Pelagius's views as heretical.

Pelagius moved to Palestine. Here he encountered another formidable enemy, Jerome, the great scholar who translated the Scriptures into the up-to-date Latin of the Vulgate Bible. He was then living in Bethlehem, and his animosity to Pelagius was not only theological but personal. Twice Pelagius was forced to defend himself before a synod.

The Eastern Church, based on Jerusalem and

Constantinople, had its own reasons for wishing to assert its independence of western authority, centred on Rome. But Augustine complained that the Briton Pelagius got off because he was able to present his case in fluent Greek, while Augustine's representative had to rely on an inadequate interpreter.

Pelagius was backed by his friend Coelestius, who may have been an Irishman from a settlement in south-west Wales. They were soon in deeper trouble. Pope Innocent I examined the charges and decided that Pelagius was innocent of all but two. He had been wrong to cast doubt on the efficacy of prayer and of infant baptism. Pelagius denied he had ever said that. Unfortunately, his supporters then attacked Jerome's monastery in Bethlehem. Innocent excommunicated Pelagius and Coelestius. A final appeal was held in Carthage before 200 bishops, representing the whole Church. Pelagius lost and his views were declared heretical. He left Jerusalem, probably for the solitude of the Egyptian desert, and died around 420. His ideas went on reverberating throughout Christendom.

## Social Conscience

Pelagius was not the only Briton to challenge the Church's thinking in those turbulent times. Other controversial writers associated with him appear to have been British. One is usually called 'the Sicilian Briton', though his country of origin is not entirely certain. The letters he wrote in the early fifth century have a startlingly modern ring. He wrote passionately about the great differences in wealth he saw. Rich people were not content with one mansion: they had to have several, expensively decked out in marble. The poor did not even have a hovel to keep out the cold or the scorching sun. 'Does God send bigger raindrops on the rich man's field than on the poor man's?' 'Don't blame inequality in wealth on the graciousness of God. Blame it instead on human sin.' And as for the parable of the rich man finding it as hard to get into heaven as a camel passing through the eye of a needle, it was no good trying to get round it by coming up with a different, ludicrous, translation. That cut no ice with God.

He had views on women. When a relative criticized him for not sending his daughter back to be taught at home, his answer was, 'Think of her as a boy. He'd be educated at boarding school.'

The blame for the Sicilian Briton's controversial book *On Riches* was laid at Pelagius's door. Pelagius denied it. In Britain, his sane ideas on free choice and responsibility continued to have a strong following long after his death.

## Germanus

Controversy had been simmering in the British Church for some time. Around 395, Victricius, Bishop of Rouen and friend of the pioneering Martin of Tours, was invited to Britain. He apologized to colleagues at home for his prolonged absence and felt sure they would forgive him when they learned that his fellow-Christians in Britain wanted him to make peace among them and that it had taken longer than he expected.

In 411, Fastidius in Britain, heard a rumour that Christians on the Continent had some strange new idea of original sin. He dismissed it as a ludicrous notion. It was clearly Augustine who was the maverick, not Pelagius.

In 429, word reached Gaul that Agricola was again stirring up Pelagianism in Britain. A British delegation asked help from the bishop of Auxerre, a former army commander, Germanus. Palladius, deacon to Pope Celestine and a man of high influence, is also credited with having a hand in the decision. Germanus and a younger bishop, Lupus, set out for Britain. We read of an open-air meeting, attended by a huge crowd, at which the Pelagians put their case. Germanus mocked their opulent dress and assumption of privilege. He accused them of a torrent of empty words. When the common people heard Germanus's eloquent answer they turned against the Pelagians and had to be restrained from violence.

31

But Germanus's biographer, though concerned to present his subject in the best possible light, is hazy about what actually happened in Britain as a result of his mission. There is no mention of bishops or church synods siding with Germanus and rejecting Pelagianism.

Instead, the story takes another turn. Germanus and Lupus went to Verulamium to deposit relics of the apostles in Alban's tomb. News reached them that a serious raiding party – a combined force of Picts and English – was on its way. It was an opportunity for Germanus to revive his old career as military commander. His arrival was delayed. First he broke his leg. Then, the street where he was staying caught fire. He lay apparently helpless, but as well-wishers rushed to rescue him, he ordered them to go off and fight the fire instead. His life was miraculously preserved, though the street was destroyed.

Eventually he made it to the British camp, where scouts had established the position of the enemy and their expected line of advance. Germanus spent the next few days exhorting the troops. He conducted a mass baptism of the war-host, then he led them out to set an ambush. As the invaders entered the defile, the newly-baptized Britons broke from cover and sent a yell of 'Alleluia!' thundering round the rocks. The other side panicked, dropped their weapons and ran.

Pelagianism was not so easily routed. Germanus paid a second visit to Britain about ten years later. This time the people are said to have thrown the Pelagians out of Britain – but the only bishops mentioned are the two from Gaul. This may indicate an alienation of the British clergy from their people, or it may mean that success eluded Germanus in eradicating these obstinately independent-thinking Britons, who believed they were the guardians of religious orthodoxy.

The English raiders returned too.

# 5

## Missionaries

### Pioneer Monks

The Sicilian Briton was not the only one to protest at conspicuous wealth. Revulsion against luxury and decadence drove many Christians to abandon town life and seek a simpler existence. The inspiration came from Egypt. Anthony was 20 years old when, around 270, he went out into the desert above the Nile and adopted the life of a hermit. He fought spiritual battles with terrifying visions of evil, but emerged a sane and influential leader and writer. Many followed his example, and Anthony organized them into communities, with an emphasis on solitary work and prayer.

The impulse spread rapidly. Some women retreated into the seclusion of their homes and led an ascetic life under a spiritual director. Others joined together in disciplined communities. There were Christian villages containing families, but many chose celibacy. At this stage, there were no recognizable orders of monks and nuns. Founders of communities each made their own Rule.

The vision of the desert hermit was adapted to western Europe by Martin of Tours, who seems to have been born into a pagan family in what is now Hungary. He joined the Roman army. In Gaul, he saw a naked beggar and was moved to cut his soldier's cloak in half to cover him. That night, in a dream, he saw Christ wearing the other half of his cloak. Soon afterwards, he was baptized. He is reported to have cleaned his slave's boots and insisted that they eat together. In time, he requested release from the army saying, 'I'm Christ's soldier; I'm not allowed to fight.'

The hermit ideal attracted him. First in Italy, then in Gaul, he sought God in solitude. He lived simply in his 'White Hut' outside Tours, and by 360 he had attracted a community of hermits around him, some living in caves. Two years later, by popular demand, he was dragged out of seclusion and made bishop of Tours. He refused to live in the bishop's comfortable town house, insisting on keeping to his hermit's hut. This did not make him popular with his fellow bishops. They complained that he was shabbily dressed and no gentleman.

But Martin was not a recluse. He travelled the countryside preaching and in this too he was a pioneer. He was one of the first to carry the Gospel to country folk and not just to the more influential town-dwellers. He visited remote communities on his donkey, refusing to ride a horse. Yet he made it clear that it was the discipline and solitude of his periods of retreat which gave him the strength for his strenuous workload for Christ.

Martin's vision spread far beyond Tours. By the end of the fourth century, the impact of the monastic movement had reached Britain. It was to affect the Church in the British Isles more profoundly than in any of the other regions of Europe.

## Ninian

The first recorded monastery in the British Isles was at Whithorn, in the kingdom of Strathclyde, north of Hadrian's Wall. It was attributed to the Briton Nynia, commonly known as Ninian. British Strathclyde lay at the outer limit of Roman influence. Ninian was probably old enough to have experienced the severe raid of Picts and Irish in 367. He is our first identifiable missionary to the Picts.

The Picts are a people whose origins we know little about. The Romans gave them the name, meaning 'Painted People' – this probably refers to their tattoos or war paint. They occupied much of what we now call Scotland, though there were Picts in Ireland too. They were related to the British, but their language and culture were not identical. Their kings seem to have traced their legitimacy through their mothers.

There is no surviving early *Life* of Ninian. Later stories tell us that he was the son of a chieftain and very tall. He visited Martin's monastery at Tours and was so impressed, both by the community and by the stone churches, that he took back a party of masons to Britain. On a southward-facing peninsula at the entrance to the Solway Firth, he built a church, part of a complex of buildings which became known as *Ad Candida Casa*, 'At the White House' (*candida* means 'shining white'). Bede suggests this was because stone buildings were unusual then, but Martin's retreat was known as 'The White Hut'. In 397, as the building was nearing completion, news of Martin's death reached Ninian. His church became known as 'Martin's House', after his hero.

The dedication of a church to a foreign saint became unusual in the Celtic regions. A 'saint' was someone who was living a holy life, there and then. Celtic churches were usually named for their founder, or the leader of the founder's community. It is sometimes possible to trace the movements of a particular man or woman through church dedications, though this method does not work with the most famous saints, like Brigid and David, who had churches dedicated to them centuries after their deaths. It also needs to be treated with caution when there is a wide scatter. These foundations might be the work of a group. The more obscure the saint, the more likely it is that the name bears witness to the man or woman living there, like Gwennap in Cornwall.

The fact that the famous Ninian's name is scattered across Scotland cannot be taken as evidence of his missionary journeys. How much of his reported travels abroad took place, we cannot be sure either. What we do know is that by the mid fifth century there was an influential monastery at Whithorn, centred around a church at which both Ninian and Martin were honoured.

The picture that emerges is that Ninian was a diocesan bishop, working in a church which was still recognizably Roman in its pattern, and that he made contact with the southern Picts in their shifting border area with Strathclyde. He converted a number of them to Christianity, but is unlikely to have penetrated deeply into the Pictish kingdoms to the north or east. He seems to have modelled his career on Martin's and to have gathered around him a community of disciples.

Like Martin, most of the Celtic saints sought a hermit's retreat. The word they used, *dysart*, springs from the inspiration of Anthony in Egypt. 'Desert' was not a negative word: Jesus felt a great need to go by himself into the wilderness to meet God. So Celtic men and women went to some deserted spot as joyfully as though to a tryst with a lover. On the shore, looking out to the Isle of Man, a narrow cave has been discovered with a number of crosses cut into the rock, along with other Christian symbols. The carvings are too late to be from Ninian's time, but there is a tradition that this was Ninian's hermitage, marked with the veneration of later pilgrims.

The story from Ninian's *Life* which gives the most vivid glimpse of his times is the incident of the student who ran away from Whithorn to escape corporal punishment. He stole Ninian's staff to help him on his way. Arriving at the beach at night, he found a coracle made of a wicker framework, and launched out in the dark, not realizing that the boat's waterproof leather covering was holed. By the time he discovered his mistake, he had been swept out to sea in this frail and leaky craft, too far to swim for the shore. When he was certain he would drown, he recollected the saint's staff and stuck it in one of the holes. To his joy, it not only kept back the water but enabled him to steer safely. Behind this miracle we catch sight of the travelling bishop, the symbolic staff of pastor and pilgrim, the sea that is highway rather than barrier, the awe of the elements.

Ninian was buried in his church at Whithorn around 432. The White House rapidly established a reputation as a co-educational centre of learning. There are tantalizing mentions from Ireland of 'Rosnat', a British monastery famed for its school. This name does not appear in British records. We do not know if Rosnat was a site now lost to us, or whether it was known in Britain by another name. Whithorn is a strong candidate.

## Patrick

While Ninian was converting the Picts, another famous pilgrim was undergoing the shattering experience which was to make him the beloved apostle of Ireland. Patrick was born somewhere near the west coast of Britain. His is almost the last we see of the upper-class British family living a Roman-style life. His grandfather had been a priest and his father Calpornius was a deacon and a town councillor, charged with collecting taxes for the Romans (there was no problem about married clergy in those days). The family lived like wealthy Romans, in a villa in the country. Patrick was given the standard Latin education – but before he could complete it, disaster struck.

A band of Irish pirates landed. They seized thousands of captives, including the 16-year-old Patrick. He was shipped across to Ireland and sold as a slave. He found himself out in the west, perhaps in County Mayo, among people who did not speak his language or know his religion. From being the privileged son of the big house with slaves, he became a slave himself, herding sheep in all weathers.

Until then, the Christianity of his parents had meant little to him. Now, in his loneliness, it was the lifeline to which he clung. He took to praying a hundred times a day, getting up early even in snow and rain. He earned himself the nickname 'the Holy Boy'.

Six years later, he had a dream: his fasting was about to be rewarded and he would return home. Obeying this prompting he ran away and covered 200 miles to the coast and a hut near the port. Perhaps he was helped by an undergound network for rescuing captured slaves. As he approached the dock, a ship had already left its berth and was preparing to sail. Patrick pleaded for a passage, but was required to swear an oath of loyalty, sealed by kissing the shipmaster's nipples. When his conscience would not allow this, the angry crew

37

turned him away. He was walking back in dejection when a voice hailed him. The captain had relented and agreed to take him on board on Patrick's terms.

Three days later they made landfall, but not according to plan. They were in an uninhabited wilderness, without food. They left the ship and struggled across country for a month, eking out their rations. The half-starved sailors reproached Patrick. Why was his God doing nothing to help them? Patrick prayed. Next moment, a herd of pigs shot across their path and soon they were feasting on pork.

Patrick was reunited with his parents, who begged him never to leave them again. But he could not forget Ireland. One night he had a vision of a man carrying an enormous stack of letters. This postman delivered one to Patrick, labelled 'The Cry of the Irish'. As he read it aloud, he heard voices he remembered crying from that wood near the western sea, 'Holy Boy, we want you to come and walk among us again.'

Patrick did his best to prepare for his vocation. He studied and became a priest, though he seems to have known none of the great books of his time besides the Bible. He probably visited Gaul. But to the end of his life, he was conscious of his rudely interrupted education. In his writings he is constantly embarrassed by his clumsy Latin. He was still a nobody in the Church, and someone else was given the mission he so much wanted.

## Mission to Ireland

When Germanus had arrived to counter British Pelagianism a few years earlier, it was said to be at the instigation of Palladius, the pope's deacon and confidential secretary. Pope Celestine now chose a man called Palladius for Ireland, possibly the same man. A pope in Rome had no authority to appoint a bishop to the British Church, but he could send one to head a missionary church in Ireland. This may have been his way of getting an anti-Pelagian into the British Isles by the back door. Palladius was commissioned first bishop to 'the Scots who believe in Christ'. The 'Scots' were originally Irish, before their migration across the water gave their name to north Britain. Ireland was never under the Roman empire, but apparently it was not entirely pagan. It had good contacts with the Continent and may have received Christian refugees from Gaul. Neither Palladius nor Patrick introduced Christianity to Ireland. There were nameless pioneers there before either of them. What Ireland appears to have lacked is an organized Church.

Palladius's mission probably concentrated on the south. It seems to have been less than a total success and little more is heard of it. Within two years, traditionally in 432 and at around the time of Ninian's death, the British Church consecrated Patrick bishop and allowed him to fulfil his heart's desire by returning to the land of his captivity. There is a poignant legend about his landing. He was determined to go to Miliucc, his former master, and redeem himself from slavery, honouring the debt he had incurred by running away, Miliucc, fearing his coming, set fire to his house and perished with all his belongings. The motivation for suicide is hard to understand, but it conjures up a moving picture of Patrick retracing the steps of his captivity, bringing both a material and spiritual ransom, only to find a heap of blackened ruins.

Centuries after his death, wonderful legends attached themselves to Patrick's mission. His first Easter coincided with the spring equinox when the king was celebrating the festival in his stronghold on the hill of Tara. Every fire in the land was put out and it was forbidden to light any flame until the king's new fire was burning. Patrick lit an Easter bonfire in sight of Tara, and druids warned that if it was not put out immediately, it would burn for ever. Patrick was sentenced to death. As king, queen and druids stormed up in their chariots, Patrick approached them singing 'Some boast of chariots, but we boast of the name of the Lord our God.' A druid was lifted up and smashed on his skull. Darkness fell, an earthquake struck. The axles of chariots locked and the horses bolted. When the chaos subsided, only the king and queen and six others were left alive.

Patrick banished all the snakes from Ireland; he used the trefoil shamrock to demonstrate the Trinity; he wrote the hymn we know as 'St Patrick's Breastplate':

> I bind unto myself today
> The strong name of the Trinity.

Alas, that was actually the work of a later and greater poet than Patrick. He would have approved of the stress on the Trinity, but the invocation of the might and majesty of creation, 'the whirling wind's tempestuous shocks', belong to a spirit that delighted in wild nature. There is no trace of this in Patrick's writings. He was brought up in the ordered Roman way. As a swineherd in the woods, he dreamed of the civilized world he had lost.

None of these inventions is necessary: Patrick's story is exciting enough in reality. It reveals a deeply human and self-doubting man who gave his life in love where he had known injustice. With Patrick's own writings we have for the first time a British Christian speaking to us about himself.

Two documents have come down to us. The first is a letter he wrote in fury to King Coroticus in Strathclyde. His soldiers had captured a party of Christians newly baptized by Patrick, still wearing their white baptismal garments and with the mark of the oil on their foreheads. Some had been killed, others taken captive. Patrick dreaded the fate of the women. The awful thing was that Coroticus and his soldiers claimed to be Christians themselves. Patrick sentenced them to excommunication, regardless of the fact that they were outside his diocese. He demanded repentance and reparation.

The other is his *Confession* – his personal statement at the end of his life, a spiritual autobiography. He clearly feels his intellectual inadequacy and the opposition of some of the clerics in Britain, from whom he had received his mandate. He tells the story of his boyhood and his escape from slavery. He regrets the lost opportunity of his unfinished schooling. He defends himself vigorously against the charge that he has used his position as bishop for his own advantage: the sons and daughters of Irish kings have joined his following, but he has directed them into an ascetic life and accepted nothing from them. Some have thrown their jewels on the altar but, to their indignation, he has returned these. He has paid princes to provide him an escort and received a poor bargain, suffering assault and imprisonment. He recalls with sorrow how, before his ordination, he confessed to a friend a secret sin committed when he was scarcely 15 years old and still in Britain. This friend betrayed his trust and made it public knowledge. Patrick still feels this hurt.

He quotes copiously from an earlier Bible than Jerome's Vulgate. He gives us an early creed, almost certainly the Rule of Faith of the British Church. it is firmly trinitarian, but contains no statement about the Son being 'of one substance' with the Father, as proclaimed at the Council of Nicaea.

He died in the land to which he gave himself willingly, after being forcibly brought there in loneliness and with loss of liberty. There is no reason to doubt him when he says that he converted thousands. Oddly enough, we do not know how or where Ireland's most famous saint died. No cult grew up immediately surrounding the tomb and relics of this humble man. Later traditions are based on Armagh.

Patrick encouraged Christian men and women of all classes to embrace an ascetic, celibate life. But he was not a monk. He founded no monasteries. The churches established by Ninian in north Britain and Patrick in northern Ireland still followed the diocesan structure, based on the authority of a bishop, with parish clergy under him.

But the situation in which they planted these churches was utterly unlike that of the Roman empire which had inspired the Romano-British pattern. Rome never conquered Ireland. There were no cities, no urban structure of civil government. It was a rural economy, a tribal system. The focal point was the king's *rath*, his earth-banked fortress. In Britain too, the Celtic pattern was never truly replaced in the outer regions. The Roman system was everywhere in collapse. People deserted the towns, which the economy could no longer support. As the Roman Church had modelled itself on the pattern of Roman civil administration, so in the century after Ninian and Patrick, a Celtic Church system evolved which better matched the social reality. The monastery became the spiritual version of the Celtic king's stronghold.

# 6

## *Arthur*

### *The English*

With the collapse of Roman rule, Britain fragmented into many kingdoms, but they were all recognizable as the *Cymry*, 'those of our land', whose memory survives in names like Cumbria. This sense of one island family, with a common, if locally differentiated, culture, was shattered by English invasions. The blame is laid at the door of Vortigern, a king of the Gloucester area ('Vortigern' is a title, meaning 'Overlord').

These English were made up of Angles, Saxons and Jutes from modern Denmark and Germany, and they had been raiding Britain for a long time. When they had seized what they wanted, they left again, establishing no substantial foothold. The Picts and the Irish were also terrorizing parts of the country. Around 430, close to the time when Ninian died and Patrick returned to Ireland, Vortigern took the ill-fated decision to set a thief to catch a thief. He hired English mercenaries to protect Britain against Pictish and Irish raids.

Three longships came, bringing a few hundred men and women. Tradition names Hengest and Horsa, 'Stallion' and 'Mare', as their leaders. With the consent of a Council of the British kingdoms, Vortigern guaranteed them food, clothing and the right to fertile land, probably on Thanet. Hengest saw opportunities for expansion and pointed out to Vortigern the advisability of calling on more of his kinsmen to defend the north. The longships multiplied.

For a time it worked. The Picts were held back, the Irish were quiet. But the other British chiefs grew restless. They renounced Vortigern's contract and told the English, 'Now that your numbers have multiplied, we can't keep feeding and clothing you all. Go home.' They should have foreseen the danger. A band of unpaid mercenaries is an invitation to disaster.

But it was civil war that broke out immediately, between Vortigern and his British opponents, led by Ambrosius. Hengest offered Vortigern reinforcements. Another 19 longships arrived and Vortigern granted the English still more land in Kent, to the consternation of its Celtic king, who knew nothing about the deal. And still the ships kept coming.

In the mid fifth century, the English struck. They burned Romano-British cities, slew their populations, killed Christian priests at their altars. Vortigern was forced to fight against the troops he had once employed. Though he had married Hengest's daughter, that did not save Britain from the 'night of the long knives'. The English had asked for a peace conference, where the two sides would meet, unarmed. But they concealed in their boots the *seax*, the long-bladed knife from which the word 'Saxon' comes. They slaughtered the leaders of Britain, sparing only Vortigern. They scarcely needed his permission to seize more land. Longships were landing along the eastern and southern coasts, no longer meeting united opposition.

Central organization was never a strong point with the Celts. Roman cities were being abandoned to weeds and forest. Kings vied jealously for power, or made uncertain alliances. The English were not organized into a single body either: they came from many parts, and spoke variations of the Germanic language. When they succeeded in conquering lands, they too set up small territories, without kings at first. But they were ruthless in their slaughter. Vast numbers of the British were killed or driven from their homes. It is impossible to say how many stayed as a slave population. By the late fifth century, the south and east of the island were ceasing to be British and were becoming English.

And still the invaders drove westward. Britons, whose leaders at least were nominally Christian, were fighting the worshippers of the Teutonic gods: Woden, who hung on the World-Tree for nine days to get wisdom; Thunor, the thunder-god with his hammer; Frig, the goddess of fertility – and many more. The future of Britain hung in the balance. Would it remain Romano-Celtic and Christian, though with a strong undercurrent of Celtic paganism? Or would it become English under the Germanic gods?

## Arthur and the Church

Names from the resistance movement flicker across the pages. One is Ambrosius Aurelianus, whose parents, it is said, 'wore the purple' and were killed in the struggle. Whatever that means, we can assume that he was from a leading Romano-British family. His father may have been the Ambrosius who led the civil war against Vortigern.

And there is Arthur. Tantalizingly, his name is not mentioned by any of the writers close to the period. But a little later, others refer to him in passing, as though they take it for granted their audience will know his story. 'He slew thousands, though he was not Arthur.' 'Where is the grave of Arthur? A mystery.' If Arthur did exist, then he was not a territorial king, but the war-leader of the Celtic Britons against the English invasion.

Tradition credits him with 12 successful battles, culminating in Mount Badon, possibly in the region of Bath, around 495. A late tradition says that Arthur went into that battle carrying a circular shield with the image of the Virgin on his shoulder. His victory was significant: for some 50 years a line held, separating the English in the lowland south and east, from the British in the more rugged north and west.

What is fascinating is the traditional depiction of the relationship between Arthur and the Church. The later romances make him an English king and the perfect Christian gentleman. Knights of his Round Table are sworn to uphold the weak against the strong and to defend women. They undertake the quest for the Holy Grail.

References from the earlier Welsh sources paint a different picture. In the *Life of Saint Cadoc*, Arthur, Cai and Bedwyr are on a hilltop playing dice when they see a woman being carried away against her will, with her father hurtling in pursuit. All our expectations lead us to suppose that Arthur will gallop to her rescue. But not a bit of it. He decides to seize her for himself and has to be restrained by his friends.

Again, Arthur is furiously pursuing a warlord who has killed three of his knights. Only St Cadoc has the courage to offer the fugitive sanctuary. For seven years the warrior remains in hiding, until someone betrays him. Arthur comes to the banks of the Usk with an army and demands compensation from the saint. He is offered 100 cows, but refuses Cadoc's gift, insisting on cattle which are red in front and white behind. Finally the saint's patience is exhausted. The cows he hands over become bundles of ferns, while the real animals return to their stalls.

In another saint's life, Arthur's greed is more pronounced. He covets the rich episcopal tunic of Padarn and demands that it be handed over to him. The bishop indignantly replies, 'This tunic is not for wicked men to wear, but for priests'. Arthur is furious. He leaves the monastery in a rage, but returns and tries to snatch the tunic. As he stamps the ground, cursing and swearing, Padarn prays for the earth to swallow him up. Next moment, Arthur is in a hole up to his chin, unable to move. He has to beg forgiveness before the saint relents and the earth returns him.

These confrontations cannot have taken place. The saints named lived after the days of Arthur. But their tone rings truer than that of the chivalrous romances about knights in shining armour. Here is the Celtic warlord, charismatic and lustful, accustomed to grabbing what he wants. Britain, including its Church, relied on such men to protect it from English conquest. Arthur, or the war-leaders he stands for, held the line so that the Celtic Church could survive.

But through these stories, the Church is also asserting its own values, the right to condemn Arthur's immorality. It was characteristic of the Celtic saints that they spoke out against anyone, regardless of rank. They were not sycophantic, upholding authority as a matter of course and turning a discreetly blind eye to its misdemeanours. They counselled the settling of feuds through blood price, not more bloodshed. They championed the disadvantaged against the aristocracy.

Britain was fighting for its life, to determine what kind of society it was going to be. In these critical conditions, the Celtic Church came to its maturity, establishing a unique identity to meet these times.

## Illtyd

Out of this violent background emerges Illtyd, the great early name leading a host of Welsh saints. He was reputed to be a cousin of Arthur's and to have served as a soldier in Arthur's army.

Illtyd, we are told, had originally no intention of becoming a monk. He was married to Trynihid. While on active service with a warlord in Mid Glamorgan, Illtyd and a party of his companions were out hunting when they got caught in a bog. Many were swallowed up, but Illtyd escaped, and the experience so shook him that he was converted. With his wife and a company of attendants he travelled south and set up camp by a river. It was a summer night. They made themselves a roof of reeds and lay down to sleep. In a dream Illtyd heard a voice telling him to part company from his wife, though she was a virtuous woman. With the dawn, he roused her and sent her, naked as she was, to see to their horses, which were pastured in the meadow. When Trynihid returned, shivering with cold, he threw her clothes at her, and told her to get dressed and leave him. She was understandably reduced to tears, but Illtyd was adamant.

Illtyd himself made his way to the house of Dyfrig, or Dubricius, who surfaces in the medieval chronicles as the archbishop who crowned King Arthur. Bishop Dyfrig gave him the ritual shaving and the habit of a monk. But Illtyd did not stay in that community. He had seen the spot he wanted and where he wished to be buried, now named Llanill-tud Fawr, or Llantwit Major, in the Vale of Glamorgan.

Meanwhile, Trynihid made her own career. She founded an oratory on the slope of a mountain and from there she offered her help to nuns and poor widows. She is reported to have made a last attempt at reconciliation. She came to Llantwit, where Illtyd was working in the fields, and asked to speak to him. He turned his back on her and refused to offer her even the hospitality due to a traveller. They never met again.

The writer is clearly inviting us to approve of Illtyd's be-haviour. As we have seen from Patrick's family, marriage was no bar to the secular priesthood. But from early on, teachers like Pelagius and Patrick encouraged their disciples, including mature married couples, to adopt celibacy. We may be seeing in this story a later generation's concern to make a sharper separa-tion between male and female monastics.

We are on more reliable ground with the reality and fame of Illtyd's school. We have evidence from his students, at first and second hand. Students flocked to Llantwit. Samson, David and Gildas are said to be among his pupils. Gildas called him 'the finest teacher of almost all Britain'. There were also lay workers who successfully farmed the valley soil for the community. When Illtyd heard that the harvests had failed in Brittany, he loaded ships with grain, including urgently needed seed-corn, and set sail with his famine relief.

Llantwit Major stands close to a Roman-style villa. Illtyd may have been a wealthy landowner who founded an early monastery on his own estate. But we need to clear from our imaginations the picture of long shady cloisters, or of Bene-dictine abbeys built like castles. The early Celtic monastery was a scattering of huts, which might have been wood or wattle or, in the far west, there were beehive structures in stone. Each monk or nun usually shared their hut with one companion, who might be their soul friend, or confessor. There was a refectory where they met together for the main meal of the day, after noon or early evening. The church was usually only a small oratory. As numbers grew, more small churches were built, rather than one larger one. A great deal of life was lived in the open air, where the light was better for working. Large services were held out of doors, with a tall cross as a focal point. Other buildings developed to meet specific needs: a guest-house for travellers, a schoolroom, a scriptorium for the copying of manuscripts, an infirmary.

Illtyd seems to have been a wiser teacher than husband. He had to cope with the idealistic excesses of his teenage pupils. Samson, at 15, was fasting to the danger of his health, and trying to maintain an attitude of prayer for two days: Illtyd counselled him to moderation. Sixteen-year-old Paul, from a rich family, was sure that the Spirit was demanding that he become a desert hermit: Illtyd gently pointed out that inner voices may come from three sources – the genuine prompting of the Holy Spirit, the temptation of the Devil, who knows our vulnerable points, or simple human desire. Later on, Samson too was troubled with the same longing, but was afraid to offend his master by asking to leave the community. Illtyd was observant enough to see that something was wrong. He got the truth out of Samson and recognized the genuine vocation to solitude which had led Illtyd to set up his own hermitage in the Hodnant valley. He arranged for him to transfer to Caldey Island, a more remote location where a small daughter monastery had recently been founded.

There is no mention of corporal punishment in Illtyd's school, or the other Welsh foundations – unlike Ninian's Whithorn, from where the student ran away in fear of a beating. But Illtyd required his monks, including those from aristocratic homes, to take a share of physical work around the monastery and in the fields. He himself was said to be farming when Trynihid came.

The sense of a close relationship with the natural world breathes through the stories of the Celtic saints. It was young Samson's turn to scare the birds off the corn and he clapped his hands at a flock of sparrows, but they only turned their heads impudently and went on eating. He ordered them off to apologize to the abbot. Illtyd, however, gave the birds his blessing and told them they would be fed daily at the monastery. In return, he asked them courteously to spare the monks' corn. Another story says that a Llantwit monk returned from work on the abbey farm to find a robin building a nest in the clean habit he wanted to change into. He kept on his dirty outdoor tunic until the fledglings had left the nest.

Celtic monasticism demanded a severe disciplining of the body and the embracing of poverty. But it did not reject the abundance of God's natural world as evil. In other times and places, the Christian Church used wild nature as the symbol of sin – but for Celtic Christians it was part of the Creator's rich generosity, providing food for the stomach and beauty for eye and ear. God had given even wild beasts the right to exist alongside humanity. The attitude of the Celtic saints was reverence and welcome.

These stories, so typical of the Celtic saints' *Lives*, may give the impression of a pastoral idyll far from the bloody battles being waged by Arthur and his like against the barbarian English. Yet this is the beloved Britain which the Celtic war-hosts were fighting and dying to protect. Men like Ambrosius and Arthur may have dreamed that they were defending Roman Britain and imperial memories of villas and cities. But those days were past, never to return. In less than a century, it was the monastic settlements which held the best of the culture and knowledge of Celtic Britain.

These monasteries cannot have been entirely peaceful havens. Refugees, fleeing from slaughter and slavery, were pouring westward, bringing their bitterness, grief and loss into the outer regions of Wales and Cornwall and north-west Britain. They took ship in mass migrations to Brittany, which owes its name to them. It was the mission of the monasteries to care for the destitute, the wounded and the bereaved. Christianity in Britain could not remain unaffected by the strength of bitterness and outrage provoked by the fugitives' stories. Among those who came to leadership in the Church, there must have been many who had themselves fled, losing homeland and relatives. It is not hard to explain the difference in attitude towards the English which was to distinguish the British Church so markedly from the Irish Church.

# 7

## Women

### Brigid

In the mid fifth century, when Patrick was preaching his last sermons in the north of Ireland, a remarkable girl was born in the kingdom of Leinster, on the central plain. Her father Dubhthac was a man of high rank and a pagan, but her mother was his Christian slave. The child was called Brigid, the name of one of the Celtic triple goddesses, revered as a giver of plenty and the patron of learning – the crafts of the poet, blacksmith, healer.

This noble Dubhthac's jealous wife had the slave woman and her infant sold to a druid household. Brigid had a Christian upbringing from her mother, but, growing up among druids, she could hardly fail to be interested in the goddess whose name she bore.

Young Brigid comes across in the stories as a spirited lass. To begin with, she was clearly a favourite with her natural father, and returned as a teenager to his house. But she had no sense of personal property. Throughout her life, she gave away anything that could be eaten, worn or bartered.

At last her father could stand it no longer. He dumped her in his chariot and drove her to the king's court, intending to sell her. While he went off to explain his business, a leper approached the chariot, begging. Brigid was just telling him she had nothing to give him when she noticed her father's sword. Impulsively she handed it over to him. When her enraged father found that she had given away his most precious possession, he dragged her in front of the king.

Brigid stuck to her principles. She told the king, 'If I had all your power, and all your wealth, and this country itself, I'd give the whole lot away to the Lord of creation.'

An offer of marriage was made to her by a highly honoured poet. Brigid refused. She said she wanted to start a community of celibate women. Whether she could actually have heard Patrick preach is doubtful, but she was clearly influenced by the ideal of ascetic life he had inspired in his disciples. As usual, she got what she wanted. She was given land for an abbey at Kildare, 'the Church of the Oak'. Her nuns ranged from princesses to slaves.

Brigid decided she needed men to do the heaviest work in a self-sufficient community, and also to celebrate the sacraments. She found Conlaed, who was heading a group of hermits nearby, and employed him as her resident bishop. The men became part of her community, with Brigid as abbess over both men and women. It was the beginning of a move which was to transform the balance of authority in the Celtic churches. Under the Roman model there was a hierarchical structure of metropolitan, bishop, priest, deacon, and other minor clergy. There was no place for women. In Britain, the earliest abbots might also have been diocesan bishops – Ninian, for example, was possibly both. At Kildare, Brigid took precedence over her bishop, Conlaed, calling on his particular skills as required – just as she needed her blacksmith, her dairywoman, her cook.

This would not have seemed revolutionary to the fifth-century Irish, who had little experience of the Christian Church. In Celtic society, girls attended schools and qualified as druids. Women fought in Celtic war-hosts until the seventh century. Women could become tribal rulers, like the fearsome Queen Maeve of Connaught. They took part in councils and were listened to with respect. It would be overstating the case to claim that they were equal with men, but Celtic women enjoyed far greater freedom than the women of Roman society.

There is a curious legend about Brigid. When she went to Bishop Mel to have the 'order of repentance' conferred upon her, he felt compelled instead to consecrate her a bishop. Since then, we are told, 'Brigid's successor is entitled to have episcopal orders and the honour due to a bishop.' Reading the *Lives* of the saints, you soon recognize predictable stories: a wild animal leads the saint to the place of hermitage, a miracle confounds an antagonistic druid or king, a scoundrel tries to cheat the saint and gets his comeuppance. Readers expected this. What you hope for is an incident which is told in no other saint's *Life*: this may be genuine biography. The claim that a female saint was a bishop is unique and startling. Some scholars dismiss this as ridiculous. Others think that the only reason it was not suppressed is because it was true.

But it is just as interesting to concentrate on Bishop Conlaed, living under the Rule of his abbess. Brigid was probably unaware of how revolutionary a step she was taking in changing the nature of ecclesiastical authority.

In another respect, Brigid must have known that she was subverting the norms of her society: Celtic paganism did not have a tradition of virginity. It is this vow of celibacy which would have been startling behaviour to her Irish contemporaries.

Brigid was not a recluse. She ranged the countryside fearlessly in her chariot, accompanied by her driver and one or two nuns. Once, a landowner blocked their way with a wall. To keep the peace, Brigid counselled making a detour, but the charioteer saw a weak point in the wall and drove at it. The chariot overturned. Brigid picked herself out of the wreckage observing, 'Short cuts make broken bones.' On another occasion, she was pitched out of the chariot and cut her head open.

Her generosity was legendary. Only a stream of miracles seems to have kept her community from starving. One cheat disguised himself as a sick man and was given a sheep out of Kildare's flock. He came back as an old beggar, and got another one. And so it went on, until he boasted of his cleverness to his friends. He arrived home to find all the sheep had taken themselves back to Brigid.

There is a song, 'Brigid's Feast':

> I should like a great lake of finest ale
> For the King of kings.
> I should like a table of the choicest food
> For the family of heaven.
> Let the ale be made from the fruits of faith,
> And the food be forgiving love.
> I should welcome the poor to my feast,
> For they are God's children.
> I should welcome the sick to my feast,
> For they are God's joy.
> Let the poor sit with Jesus at the highest place
> And the sick dance with the angels.
>
> (Traditional, in Toulson, *The Celtic Year*)

Patrick is said to have travelled Ireland with his 'family': a champion to protect him and carry him across fords, a judge, a handbell-ringer, a chaplain carrying his Bible, embroideresses and teachers of needlework, blacksmiths, goldsmiths, carpenters and masons. An array of skilled workers, male and female, contributed their artistry and scholarship in the service of the young Church. The Celtic saints adopted lives of personal simplicity, but devoted all the glory of Celtic art and craftsmanship to the worship of God.

So it was at Kildare. In the tradition of her namesake goddess, Brigid became the patron of poets, smiths and healers. Conlaed, her bishop, was a skilled smith, making altar vessels for the church at Kildare, ornamented with interlacing Celtic patterns. One later visitor described a beautiful illuminated *Book of Kildare*, whose gilded and coloured pages cast enchantment over him as he turned them.

Within a century, a church was built at Kildare which was unusual for its size and beauty. The walls were painted with pictures and there would have been richly embroidered hangings. The body of the church was partitioned, to segregate male and female worshippers, with another wooden screen separating the clergy at the east end. Men and women entered this area through separate doors to receive communion. Here, Brigid and Conlaed were buried, with gold and silver crowns hanging over them.

Centuries after Brigid's death there was a tradition of a perpetual fire kept burning at Kildare. Nineteen nuns tended it, taking a day and a night each. But on the twentieth night the words were spoken, 'Brigid, tend your own fire tonight.' In the morning it would still be glowing. Even in her lifetime, Brigid was revered almost as a goddess. She was associated with arts and learning and the work of the dairy. A tradition grew up that she served as midwife and wet-nurse to the Christ-child and accompanied the Holy Family on the flight to Egypt. She is invoked in prayers as 'Mary of the Gael'.

## Partnership and Celibacy

Brigid's abbey was not unique. Patrick's writings suggest that more women disciples than men turned to the ascetic life. Faencha and Darerca also had famous houses. Indeed, women founded the most prominent monastic communities in early Christian Ireland. These were not true double houses, in the sense of being equal communities of men and women under one abbess. The fifth-century Irish monks, fewer in number than the nuns, often carried out their religious vocation in cells associated with these thriving women's communities.

Despite this prominent role, women were not priests. But there is an incident which strikes an interestingly modern note. Not long after Brigid's time, in the middle of the sixth century, Bishop Melaine of Rennes sent out a letter to his Breton priests ordering them to 'stop wandering from house to house, celebrating Mass on portable altars and accompanied by women who administer the chalice'. Brittany had been inundated by refugees who crossed the Channel from Britain, fleeing the yellow plague or the English. The use of portable altars for rural congregations is well attested in the British Isles and it is reasonable to suppose that this involvement of women in the Eucharist, found in the early Eastern Church too, was also practised there.

It should not be assumed that these nuns only devoted their working hours to domestic tasks, the dairy, caring for the sick and stitching magnificent church embroidery. They did all these things – but were also academic students, teachers and scribes. Darlugdach, Brigid's cell-mate and successor at Kildare, sailed to Strathclyde to study at Whithorn. Darerca, who founded monasteries in Ireland at about the same time as Brigid, is also known as Mo-ninna. This may mean that she too was a pupil at Ninian's Whithorn. The earliest British monastic schools we know of, Ninian's and Illtyd's, were coeducational.

In the transition from a pagan society, where marriage partners were easily changed and sexual freedom permitted, to Christian monasticism, there were, not surprisingly, occasional scandals. Darlugdach confessed to her cell-mate Brigid her struggle against the temptation to steal from their shared bed and meet her lover.

Around 550, Drusticc, a Pictish princess, was a student at Whithorn. She fell in love with a fellow-student, Rioc, whose name suggests he was British. She bribed another student, the Irishman Finnian, who later founded a great monastery at Moville, to bring Rioc to her bed. Instead, he produced an Irish friend. Then she tried to seduce Finnian himself and they were both expelled. Finnian was flogged and there was a student uprising to reinstate him. Since Pictish kings claimed succession through their mothers, possibly after a temporary marriage, there could have been political, as well as moral, implications.

The penitentials of the monasteries make provision for a wide range of sexual transgressions. But the greater reality is that over the next centuries thousands of men and women flocked into monasteries, embracing a chaste life. Some were widowed, others were married people past the age of warfare and childbearing. Many were children offered by their parents. But large numbers were young men and women freely choosing a lifetime of celibacy.

The pattern set by Brigid's community of monks and nuns was to be repeated many times. In other places and in the following centuries, separation between the sexes was more strictly enforced. The story of Illtyd rejecting his wife Trynihid was first told by a later generation. A similar story tells how Justinian landed on Ramsey Island, off the Pembrokeshire coast, to make a hermitage. He found Honarius already there, living a life of prayer with his sister and her maid. Justinian insisted on expelling the two women to the mainland, then he and Honarius settled down to live harmoniously together.

But other stories reach a different understanding. In Brigid's time, Docco and Kew, brother and sister, sailed from Gwent to land on the north coast of Cornwall near Wadebridge. Docco refused to let his sister near his hermitage, until one day he came upon her scolding a savage wild boar and making it behave itself. Docco was impressed. He resumed conversations with Kew and found her full of virtue and holiness.

## Pioneering Women

Cornwall is full of churches dedicated to Celtic saints, women and men. Frequently in the stories, they float there from Ireland or Wales on a leaf or millstone. Yet the legends are grounded in reality. These dedications record courageous journeys.

Celtic holy women did not lead lives of seclusion. They founded monasteries, decided the Rule that would govern them, assisted the poor and the sick, encouraged arts and craftsmanship, established schools. Many of the great male saints of the next century were educated by women.

Faencha, like Brigid, founded her monastery in late fifth-century Ireland – and she was not a woman to be intimidated by gender or status. One day, the young chieftain Enda and his warriors came riding home from a battle, roaring a triumph-song and probably swinging bloody heads from their saddles. Faencha erupted from her cell in front of them: 'That horrible caterwauling doesn't spring from the tomb of Christ. You're a murderer.' 'It's my job to defend my father's inheritance and fight our enemies,' protested the indignant Enda. 'Your father's in hell. All he left you is crime and wickedness,' she retorted.

This intrepid woman, living like the poorest peasant, made a startling impression on the young warlord. Enda was converted, joined her community and adopted the same lifestyle.

But Faencha was not totally convinced. Soon afterwards, Enda was at work helping to build their growing monastery when he realized that his former war-band was being attacked by a cattle-rustling gang. Faencha saw the young chief throw down the plank he was carrying – and she moved swiftly to forestall him: 'You must leave Ireland, or the things of this world are bound to seduce you.'

She ordered him to Whithorn in Britain. 'How long have I got to stay there?' he asked. 'Until I get good reports of you,' came the crisp reply. Enda came back a changed man and founded a monastery on Inishmore, largest of the offshore Aran Islands, with a particularly strict Rule.

In the next generation, we read of Brendan, the navigator saint, going often to the abbess Ita, who is said to have slept on the bare earth and to have washed her hands after handling money. She was not a priest, but she was clearly Brendan's soul friend, giving him both spiritual counselling and practical advice.

A monk, doggedly carrying out a task Brendan had set him, was in danger from the rising tide. A brother ran to warn Brendan, who impatiently replied, 'If you're so worried about him, take his place yourself.' The boy did and drowned. The Church asked Ita to set Brendan's penance, and she sent him into temporary exile from Ireland. When Brendan was planning an Atlantic exploration, Ita, it is said, advised him how to construct his ship.

These early women's stories ring with confident authority and with a cheerful disregard for their own comfort or safety.

# 8

## Monasteries

### Gildas

Arthur's victory at Mount Badon at the end of the fifth century won a period of grace for western Britain. But it lasted for little more than a generation. The breaking-up of the Round Table in the Arthurian romances is symbolic of what actually happened. In Celtic society there was fierce local pride – and a century after the unifying Roman empire withdrew, the British kingdoms were at each other's throats, just as much as they were fighting the English. One monk watched the moral degeneration in the royal families with helpless rage. Around 538, he took up his pen in an astonishing diatribe against the rulers and secular clergy.

Gildas was born in the kingdom of Strathclyde, and may have been a Pict. His family moved to the island of Mon, or Anglesey, and Gildas went further south to become one of many great churchmen who studied at Illtyd's school at Llantwit. The kings he names are from Wales and the south west.

His book, *The Ruin of Britain*, begins with a survey of the Roman conquest, the martyrdom of Christians like Alban, the onslaught of the Irish and the Picts and the flight from the towns as imperial rule collapsed. He tells how Vortigern, whom he calls only 'the proud tyrant', invited English warbands into Britain and he assigns the first victories against them to Ambrosius Aurelianus. He moves to the battle of Mount Badon, recording that it took place in the year of his own birth, but he does not tell us who led the British troops that day. He does not mention Arthur. (There is a Welsh

59

tradition that Arthur killed Gildas's brother Huail, a detested pirate, and that Gildas demanded blood money from him – such animosity may account for the omission.)

Gildas gets into his stride when he reaches his own sixth century. What good has victory brought? 'Britain has kings, but they are tyrants. She has judges, but all of them wicked.' He makes a catalogue of their crimes, starting with Constantine of Dumnonia in the south west. This 'tyrant cub of the filthy lioness' has murdered two young princes in their mother's presence, clothing the sanctuary of the church, their spiritual mother, in a 'purple cloak' of blood. Maelgwn of North Wales is accused of vowing to be a monk, then going back on his vows to marry, and finally murdering his wife and nephew in order to marry the nephew's widow. And so on. He marshals a huge body of biblical evidence to condemn them all. At the end of this, he confesses himself exhausted, like a sailor who 'has been tossed about on the waves for so long and has rowed himself into the harbour he longed for at last'.

But he forces himself on, turning his anger on the clergy. The priests are fools, the ministers are shameless, the clerics are only out for what they can grab. In place of shepherds, the Church has wolves. They buy their posts, and are only concerned with profit and filling their own bellies. Far from helping poor people, the clergy look with disgust at them, as though they were hideous snakes – but they respect the rich, as if they were angels from heaven. These priests are so fat that their voices are as hoarse as bellowing bulls.

A century earlier, Germanus had accused the Pelagian party of being urbane, showily dressed, out of touch with the common people – though this did not accord with the social gospel of Pelagius's disciples. Gildas was charged with Pelagianism himself, and is not free of elitism. But he is here condemning real corruption in the non-monastic, or 'secular', Church. There were many reasons why the movement to the monasteries swelled to a flood in the sixth century. The decadence of the British secular religious establishment was clearly one.

There were other motives. With the collapse of Roman administration in Britain, roads became unsafe, making wide-scale trade impractical. Towns lost agricultural supplies from the countryside, and fell into ruin. Famines occurred, unde-fended country villas were abandoned, government rents and taxes were not collected. With no market for the stonemason, the potter, the skilled toolmaker, apprentices were not taken on and crafts learned from the Romans were lost. There was a reversion to subsistence farming, producing only enough surplus to support the chief's warriors and provide his patronage for traditional Celtic crafts. In the midst of this upheaval, the monasteries offered stable and economically viable communities. These were the places to find schooling, medicine, hospitality, worship. They could offer opportunity for men and women, and safeguard knowledge.

## Samson in Wales

Samson was a contemporary of Gildas, and was another of Illtyd's pupils. His biography was written by a disciple, close enough to his death to contain accurate information. He was taken to the monastery school at the age of five, where his father made a gift of the dried carcase of a stag, a salmon and a honeycomb. With great speed the child learned his alphabet, probably using 20 little tiles with a letter on each, and progres-sing to writing on wax tablets. Illtyd was reputed to be 'the most learned of all the Britons'. His pupils studied the Scrip-tures, but also philosophy, rhetoric, grammar, geometry and arithmetic.

The teenage Samson's wish to find a quieter retreat for intense communion with God was heightened by danger at Llantwit. Samson was swiftly made deacon, and then priest, long before the usual age of 30. Illtyd had two nephews, one of them a priest. They had assumed that one of them would succeed their uncle as abbot, and looked with alarm at this talented and devout young monk whom Illtyd favoured. The priest was the abbey's cellarer, responsible for food and drink, so they plotted to poison Samson. First, they tried their herbal potion on the cat, which leaped into the air and fell dead. But seeing Samson drink his draught unharmed, the cellarer repented. His brother did not. In the triumphant manner of these stories, on the next Sunday, as Samson was officiating at communion, the sinner collapsed at the altar rail, stripping off his clothes, biting his lips and ranting at the brethren. Strong monks bound him and carried him outside, where he finally confessed.

The legend has its basis in a monastic pattern adopted from Celtic chieftainship. Abbots were often of the royal clan, potential chiefs themselves. The *co-arb*, or heir, was designated in the lifetime of the abbot, usually from the founder's own family.

Samson was sent to Caldey Island, where Piro was heading a new community. If he had hoped to find a greater sanctity there, he was destined to be disappointed. One night, Abbot Piro was drunk. Rolling back to his cell in the dark, he tumbled into a pit. Though the brothers heard his yells and pulled him out, he died before morning. Samson was made abbot, but it only lasted a year. He was unable to reform the community. The brothers regarded him as an oddity, calling him a hermit rather than a monk like themselves. He is said to have slept on his feet, leaning against a wall, and made a point of fasting 'amid feasts of plenty and flowing bowls'. Though he was not a total abstainer, nobody ever saw him drunk.

It would be unfair to dismiss Piro as completely unspiritual because of the manner of his death. In his life, he reproved Samson for lack of charity. Samson had received a message that his father was dying, but he refused to return home, saying that God could heal his father without Samson's attendance. Abbot Piro reproached him for his callousness: he must cultivate a spiritual harvest in the family where he himself had grown.

The remorseful Samson set out in a horse and cart, with a young companion. On the way, they were attacked by a demented pagan holy woman, with shaggy grey hair and a red tunic, brandishing a bloody trident. The young deacon let go of the horse's head and fled, with the elderly sorceress in pursuit, but was half dead before Samson caught up. Samson yelled at the sorceress to stop. She told him that she was one of nine sisters, who was bound to this wood by the order of her dead husband. When she refused to heal the young monk or to repent, Samson cursed her and she immediately died of a heart attack. The Church put Samson on trial for that curse, but exonerated him.

Samson was reunited with his family. His father recovered and he, Samson's mother and three brothers, divided the bulk of their wealth between the poor and the Church, and embraced the monastic life. There remained a small sister, who showed no love for God. Samson was concerned, but left orders that the family should continue to support her.

## Diversity

In Ireland, Enda, the wild young chieftain sent to Whithorn by Faencha, came back a reformed character. He asked King Angus of Munster to grant him one of the uninhabited Aran Islands off the west coast – but Angus protested that Patrick had told him to give the Church good agricultural land near the court. A tension was developing between the tribal function of the monasteries, replacing the druid colleges, and this more extreme wing of asceticism. Enda got his island where the Atlantic sweeps into Galway Bay, and set up a Rule with a severe discipline.

Monastic and secular churches alike had to operate with the permission of the local ruler. Saints ranged across boundaries and frequently established monasteries outside their own native area. But this required land, and land could only be granted by the chief. What emerged was a pattern of local churches, each serving a particular kingdom, and reaching different decisions. There was interchange and consultation between them, and strong cross-border loyalties between abbeys having the same founder. But different parts of these islands did not always agree. There was no unified Celtic Church.

# Schools

Finnian founded the first great Irish monastic college at Clonard, near the centre of Ireland, around 530. Unlike the more remote Aran Islands, Clonard stood only 20 miles from the court and 20 from Brigid's Kildare. Finnian's first generation of students went out to start a galaxy of other monasteries: Ciaran at Clonmacnois, Columba at Derry, Brendan at Clonfert, Kevin at Glendalough, Comgall at Bangor, and a host more. With the same exuberance as the Celtic warriors who had flung themselves into battle against tremendous odds, the Celtic monks and nuns threw themselves into the extreme demands of monastic life and learning.

From pre-Christian times there had been druid and bardic schools, requiring at least 12 years' study. Their teaching and learning was entirely oral, and huge repertoires of wisdom, stories, songs and genealogies were committed to memory. Celtic languages had no written form, though Latin and Greek writing were known, even in pre-Christian Ireland. A script known as 'Ogham' was developed, a code of straight lines, set at angles, scored upon stones or wood, but it was suitable only for inscriptions, not for detailed texts.

When the Celtic monasteries took over as tribal schools, they introduced the revolutionary practice of reading and copying manuscripts. Unwieldy scrolls had already given way to codices – pages encased between book covers – and for those who had renounced earthly wealth, these books were their greatest treasures. Foremost, of course, were the biblical books. There were at this time no complete Bibles, since in handwritten form they would have been of enormous size. The most popular separate volumes were the Gospels and the Psalter, but copies of all the other Old and New Testament books were made. Latin was the standard language, but Greek was known, and at Ciaran's Clonmacnois some of the gravestones are inscribed in Hebrew. There were commentaries on the Scriptures, many of them copies of the early Fathers' work. Celtic scholars added more. Ninian of Whithorn contributed a famous *Meditation on the Psalms of*

*David*. There were hymns and prayers. Columba was a poet both in Latin and Irish. Abbots drew up Penitentials for a list of sins. Besides religious works, they had a huge repertoire of learning from the pre-Christian past, and enriched their libraries with the works of Cicero, Horace and Virgil. They taught the classical curriculum, from philosophy to geometry. Brendan the navigator studied astronomy at Clonard.

Students like Finnian and Darlugdach had to cross to Britain to extend their higher education – indeed, the stories of the Church in these two islands interlace like Celtic knotwork. A stream of Irish men and women returned from Whithorn and the Welsh foundations, bringing treasures of learning. They copied old texts, wrote new ones, taught others. With Britain under increasing pressure from barbarian inroads, Ireland forged ahead. In the mid sixth century the tide turned, and those who sought the best teaching flocked to Ireland. They did not all come from Britain. Shiploads of Continental students were reported on the Shannon. Some English names appear. With a generosity which puts our own century to shame, Irish schools offered foreign students free board and teaching, and the loan of books. Accounts of the great monasteries of Clonard, Bangor and Clonmacnois may be exaggerated, but with monks, nuns, students and lay workers, some numbered their occupants in thousands.

In Ninian and Illtyd's time, all the texts were in Latin, Greek or Hebrew. Before the end of the sixth century, a great step forward was taken. Authors began to write works in Irish, making it the first medieval European language to appear in written form.

## Monastery and Society

It is said that, in Ninian's time, the estate of Whithorn was so large that it took him more than a day to ride out to the boundary. There was much farm work to be done. Some monasteries employed lay workers, or even kept slaves – but in most, monks and nuns took a share in the work, including those born princes. At Clonard, the first pupils took it in turns to provide the daily meal. Brigid is associated with dairy work, which she had done as a slave. At Killaloe, one of Molua's monks grumbled that the task of cutting thistles was beneath him; the abbot simply picked up a sickle and set to work himself.

Lay people made gifts of food, cloth, or their children. Monasteries were excused rents and taxes (sometimes a cause of friction), and monks and nuns were excused military service. The monastery was expected to make some return to society. Besides education and health, their role was to pray for the prosperity of the land, for the king and his warriors, and to curse the kingdom's enemies. There was a strong belief in the efficacy of curses; even a satirical poem could cause physical wounds. In the early seventh century, hundreds of monks from Bangor-ys-Coed were massacred as they prayed on the side of the British war-host.

## Worship

But the chief work of a monastery was worship.

There is a temptation to read of something happening in one Celtic monastery and assume that it holds good for every monastery, in all Celtic lands, in every century. This misses the point that these abbots were pioneers, literally making the Rules up as they went along. There was considerable variation, with founders devising the Rule for their own abbey, under the guidance of a spiritual director. Daughter houses often followed the mother abbey, and there was a constant interchange of people and ideas, but no uniformity. Benedict and Scholastica were already setting up houses under the Benedictine Rule in Italy, but this had not yet reached the British Isles. Some monks moved from one monastery to another to find the Rule they preferred.

At one extreme was Perpetual Praise. A large monastery might have choirs working shifts, so there was never a time when God was not being praised. More typically there were services every three hours. Nuns and monks kept vigil to ring the bell at night. The Celtic churches were in love with the Psalms. In seventh-century Bangor, the number of psalms sung at a service ranged from three at morning worship to 75 at the weekend on a long winter's night. In some cases, monks who could not be in church halted wherever they were working, and raised their voices in the same psalm.

And, of course, there were private devotions too. Some set themselves to recite the whole Psalter every day. Time and again we hear of Celtic saints standing in water to pray. A favourite legend is of the holy man who endures this, only to return to the abbey and be struck rigid with cold. A boy, destined to become a famous saint himself, is sent to fetch live coals to warm him and carries the fire back in his tunic, unharmed.

Prayer was made standing with uplifted hands, or, less often, prostrate. A self-imposed discipline was to pray for hours with arms extended like the cross. Kevin of Glendalough is said to have stood so long in prayer that a blackbird nested in his hands.

Fundamental to Celtic spiritual discipline was the soul friend, in an era when private confession was unusual elsewhere. It was said that 'Anyone without a soul-friend is like a body without a head.' A soul friend heard your confession, decided your penance, might share your cell. This was not an anonymous voice from behind a screen, but the deeply personal relationship of spiritual director. Penance must be done before absolution was given.

In the pagan Celtic tales, adjective is heaped upon colourful adjective to evoke the warrior Cu Chulainn's battle-aspect or the enchanted Land of the Ever-Young. This love of exaggeration wrote itself into the Celtic liturgy. Services were in Latin, but a particularly Celtic style developed. As in the cross-Channel Gallican Church, there was a flowery language, a heaping together of collects, and colourful rites more extreme than in the Roman tradition.

The Eucharist, known as the 'Offering', was celebrated weekly and on feast days. There were little wattle oratories, where a local hermit led a few peasant families in worship once a week. In the richer abbeys, there was silver and gold workmanship for the altar, Gospel books and Psalters, with illuminated letters glowing from the page. Ecclesiastical embroiderers contributed vestments and altar hangings. Lighted torches might have accompanied the reading of the Gospel.

## Discipline

Such glory was for God. In their personal lives, monks and nuns often chose stark simplicity. Typical dress was a long white undergarment, with a tunic of undyed wool. But some wore leather and others retained their secular dress, with some functional jewellery. There was a hooded cloak, gloves, and sandals or boots. As they travelled, they carried leather satchels for their few necessities and their precious books. Often they took a harp, though the short-tempered eighth-century hermit Mael-ruain, founder of the Culdee revival of asceticism (see Chapter 15), forbade music in his hearing.

It was an old Celtic custom that a warrior was shaved by his lord when he entered his service. Monks too had their hair shaved as a sign of service to their Lord. The Celtic monks' tonsure, a point of fierce contention later, possibly followed the same pattern as that of the druids – and probably consisted in shaving the front half of the skull and leaving the hair behind long. The entry of a nun to God's service was symbolized by her receiving a veil.

Diet was often meagre, though with wide variations. There was usually one main meal, taken after the noon service or in the early evening. Few ate meat, though it might be provided for guests. Hard bread, vegetables, eggs and fish were normal fare. Wednesdays and Fridays were fast days, but the laws of hospitality might require this to be broken if a guest arrived. More fasting was laid down as a penance for sins. Ale was not shunned. The story of Piro's death, and frequent mention of drunkenness in the Penitentials, bear witness to an old Celtic problem.

# David

David took asceticism to greater extremes. His father was said to be Sant, which means 'saint', and his mother Non, or 'nun' – perhaps it was a friendship between theological students which got out of hand. She fled to bear her baby in secret in a cliff-top cottage one stormy night.

David was sent to a Welsh monastic school under Paulinus, possibly a pupil of Germanus. Leadership came early, when his abbot died. It is said that Gildas, who had had a liberal education under Illtyd, visited the monastery near Cardigan Bay and tried to take over, but the Church decided in David's favour.

In time, David grew disillusioned with that abbey. The story says that he and his disciples moved on, but the smoke of their camp-fire was seen by Boia, an Irish brigand who was terrorizing the neighbourhood. He stormed up to David's settlement and ordered him to leave. David reasoned with him and Boia took himself off, but his wife was made of stronger stuff. She ordered her women to strip themselves naked and bathe in full view of David's monks. They protested to him that they could not possibly follow a life of prayer in the face of such daily provocation. David assured them that if they took no notice, the women would eventually get tired of it. The brigand's wife next made ritual sacrifice to her gods. She made her stepdaughter pick nuts, then took the girl's head in her lap, sheared off her hair and cut her throat. Even this failed to shift David, and she had to flee from her husband's wrath. Another shipload of pirates landed and killed Boia. David got his monastery, now known as St David's, at Menevia on the south-west tip of Wales.

Many nuns and monks are said to have slept on the ground, pillowed their heads on a stone and practised self-flagellation. There is a poem giving God's approval of:

> the cells that freeze
> the thin pale monk upon his knees.

David's regime was still harsher. He forbade alcohol, earning himself the nickname 'the Water Man'. He kept his monks labouring through the daylight hours, and then reading, writing and praying in the evening. They harnessed themselves to the plough instead of oxen, and dressed in hides. Conversation was frowned on and obedience strictly enforced. He abhorred the liberal classical curriculum, with its pagan philosophers; his school taught only scriptural subjects. It produced no great scholars. Those who wished to join him were kept waiting outside the gate for ten days, while the brothers inside hurled insults at them.

Gildas, who had himself condemned murderous kings and decadent priests in *The Ruin of Britain*, disapproved. He wrote letters ridiculing those who boasted of fasting on dry bread and water but indulged in hatred and backbiting. He accused 'those who haul ploughs' of presumption and pride. He cautioned against allowing monks to change their monastery just because the old one was relaxed about using animals and vehicles. There is no doubt whom he had in mind.

Gildas's own Penitential shows that discipline was needed. There are penalties for a monk too drunk to sing the Psalms, and for one who overeats so much that he vomits up the sacred host. But he stood for moderation, even if he expressed it intemperately. His penalty for masturbation is three hours' standing vigil in the night, but only if the monk's health is strong and the monastery well supplied with beer and meat. If the diet is poor, the penance is reduced to singing 30 psalms or doing extra work.

Gildas was an aristocrat, as were most Welsh abbots. David, untypically, came from plebeian stock. Gildas scoffed at David's type for preferring slaves to masters and common people to kings, 'as though the stars in the sky and the angels in heaven were all equal'. He complained that they exalted the monk's cell above the church. Gildas stands at the transition between the old diocesan Roman Church and the growing power of the Celtic abbeys.

# Cadoc

The difference in social outlook is even more marked with Cadoc. He inherited from his father both a kingdom and an abbey in south Wales, with tenants providing income. It was said he maintained not only 100 clergy and 100 workmen, but also 100 warriors on the hillfort above. His abbey fed poor men, widows, squires, servants and guests.

A local ruffian's war-band once raided the monastery and made off with food and drink. Cadoc sent monks to creep up on them while they were gorged and drunk and, in an echo of the ritual insult in an old Welsh myth, ordered them to shave half the heads of the sleeping brigands and slash off the ears and lips of their horses with razors. It is this same colourful biography which gives Cadoc victory over a presumptuous Arthur. The gist of this tradition is clear: Cadoc was not a man to mess with.

The tension between David and these aristocratic abbots is said to have come to a head at the Synod of Brefi. David's supporters brought a charge, probably of Pelagianism, against Gildas and Cadoc. At first David refused to attend, having turned his back on the sinful world outside his monastery. A deputation was despatched to fetch him and he won the case. Cadoc was furious that the Synod had been held while he was abroad. As an injured party, he began a ritual fast against David, an action which was believed to cause real harm. With some difficulty he was persuaded that his action lacked Christian charity. In fact, the Synod of Brefi was probably more about penance than Pelagianism, but the story shows that debate was still going on.

Sentimentality about the Celtic churches should be tempered by the fact that monks did sometimes take up weapons. Rival abbeys even fought each other. The warlike Celts did not undergo a complete personality change when they entered the abbeys: they simply channelled their energy in a different direction. In Ireland, it was the pioneer nuns, Faencha, Darerca, Brigid and Ita, who were most vocal in their appeals for peace.

## Hermits

At the other end of the scale from Cadoc's ecclesiastical court were the monks who perched their beehive huts and little oratory on the crags of Skellig Michael, precipitous rocks eight miles out in the Atlantic off the Kerry coast. We delight in their reckless courage, as well as in the spiritual peace of Bardsey Island or Kevin's woodland Glendalough, the 'Valley of the Lakes'. It is easy to jump to the conclusion that the spirit of Celtic monasticism is escape from the human world into wild nature. That would be a misunderstanding. Though they set themselves up as Christian strongholds, few monasteries were as isolated as all that. The sea was a highway, no more difficult and dangerous to negotiate than most land journeys. Major abbeys were usually situated within easy reach of the royal centre. Abbots were frequent visitors at the king's court to offer advice or warnings. Monks and nuns undertook long journeys at home and voyages abroad, and received visitors from far afield.

Yet the hermit's life held a powerful attraction. There are later poems rhapsodizing about life with only the blackbird's song and the rushing stream for company, and with cresses and eggs to eat. Worshipping under sheltering boughs, one poet celebrates 'God the Thatcher'. Powerful abbots administering large monasteries might spend the whole of Lent in a solitary retreat. Kevin's hermitage was a Bronze Age barrow on a spur of rock high above the lough. Columba left Iona to fast on the island of Hinba. In the seventh century, Aidan of Lindisfarne chose a rocky islet of Inner Farne. The solitary life demanded spiritual maturity: those who sought it usually had to work a period of probation in the community first.

The pursuit of solitude seldom worked. Time and again we read of saints who tried to retreat to a hermitage – but their visible holiness was so apparent people flocked out into the wilderness after them. This sometimes resulted in a new community.

# Retreat

Beuno had another reason for escaping from the world around him. One day, out walking by the Severn at Welshpool, he heard a huntsman on the other bank shouting to his hounds in English. It was more than Beuno could bear – evidence of the invasion which was inflicting such hurt on his fellow Britons. He told his community, 'Get dressed and put on your shoes. Those foreigners across the Severn are about to take over our land too.' He retreated by degrees to the coast of the Lleyn peninsula, the far north west of Wales. It is said that Beuno planted an acorn beside his father's grave which grew into a spreading oak, one of whose branches took root in the ground. Only the Welsh could walk safely under that arch. For the English, it brought death.

Christian Britain was losing ground, in desperate danger. But its schools had lit a torch which passed beyond its shores. The twin flames of salvation and scholarship were burning now in the Irish Church.

# 9

## *Pilgrimage*

### *The Pilgrim Vision*

We used to call the period following the retreat of the Romans after 410, 'the Dark Ages,' seeing the British Isles as cut off from the rest of Europe, the light of its culture dying, to emerge into the daylight again with the coming of the Normans in the eleventh century. Yet in the western regions culture was not only alive but was moving towards new heights of artistic expression. And the inhabitants of the British Isles were certainly not cut off from the rest of the world.

Given the difficulties and dangers of travel, it seems astonishing that they should undertake journeys as far as Rome or Iceland, but they did. They were inspired by a variety of motives, of which the conventional pilgrimage, to a religious site hallowed by the past, was only one. Indeed, the story of a saint's journey to Rome may indicate no more than that a later generation wished to claim the authority of Rome for the saint's actions. Yet such journeys were made. The scale of them was sufficient to drive one Irish poet to warn, 'To travel to Rome is much trouble for little profit. Unless you take the King you are seeking with you, you won't find him there.'

The distinctively Celtic vision of pilgrimage is very different. It is not a journey into the Christian past, but the adventure of launching oneself out into the unknown.

# Brendan

Celtic literature delights in miraculous odysseys – the pagan *Voyage of Bran*, the secular *Voyage of Maelduin*. Celtic Christianity's great navigator is Brendan, who died around 575. *The Voyage of St Brendan* was written centuries after his death, though based on an earlier document. It is wonderfully specific in many of its details, with incidents paralleled nowhere else in the *Lives* of the saints.

Brendan's voyage is inspired by the visit of a monk who has discovered the Island of Promise of the Saints. Celtic mythology had a dream of marvellous islands in the western ocean, ruled by fairy women, whose trees were hung with silver blossom and golden fruit. There was hunting and fighting and horse-racing by day, feasting and music at night. All hurts were healed and no one ever grew old. For Christians, it became Paradise.

Fourteen monks volunteered to join Brendan's expedition. The building and provisioning of their ship is given close attention. Tanned skins were stretched over a wooden framework and the seams caulked with sheep-fat. Spare hides and grease were loaded on board for running repairs, along with provisions for 40 days.

They sailed off merrily until the wind dropped, and then rowed on until they were exhausted. Brendan told them to ship their oars, hoist sail, and wait for God to take them where he would. Seeing an island, they disembarked, lit a fire and were terrified when the ground heaved to life under them. They had landed on a whale. They sailed through a shimmering canopy to a column of crystal. They were driven off a barren island by a red-faced smith who seized blazing slag with tongs and hurled it at the ship. Stones hit the water hissing, 'like a cauldron of stew boiling over a good fire', and the air was foul with rotten stench. A volcano erupted, 'vomiting flames sky-high', while glowing rock poured down black cliffs to the shore.

Shoals of sea creatures swayed over the sea-bed 'like a city on the march', and the crew begged Brendan to say the Eucharist silently, so as not to provoke them to attack. But with a true Celtic celebration of nature, Brendan laughed, 'Isn't Jesus Christ Lord of creation?' – and bellowed the service at the top of his voice. The creatures broke surface and swam round the ship until he had finished. When the voyagers next landed, they found fruit like grapes growing everywhere.

After seven years like this, they were led on a new course, into a bank of fog. They sailed out into brilliant light to find an island where every plant was in flower, every tree bore fruit and the ground was formed of precious jewels. On the bank of a vast river a young man greeted them each by name, with a kiss. He told them they had found their Land of Promise; now it was time to go home.

Reality and vision interlace. There is evidence that Brendan did reach the Hebrides. It is easy to picture the whales, icebergs, volcanoes of the North Atlantic. In 1976 Tim Severin constructed a ship like Brendan's and demonstrated that it could indeed sail to North America.

But what it tells us about a voyage of the spirit is just as significant. Hermits who pushed themselves through extreme discipline to ecstatic communion with God, scholars who conceived that it was possible to write the word of God in their own language, artists who gave us glorious manuscripts in defiance of the barbarism threatening their society, were all embarked on their own odysseys of faith.

The historical Brendan founded many communities, even into his seventies, notably Clonfert in central Ireland, one of the great teaching abbeys. He died in the arms of his sister Brig, in her abbey overlooking the Atlantic.

## Voyages of Faith

The stories of the saints swarm with shorter voyages, with transforming consequences. Patrick is said to have brought the pirate Maughold to repentance. As penance, he ordered him to set sail without oars or rudder. Maughold was washed up on the Isle of Man, where the church overlooking the landing place bears his name.

Cornwall is thickly sown with Celtic saints. Their sacred history is recorded in the names of churches, holy wells and villages. Many sailed from Ireland or Wales. Ia is said to have crossed on an enormous leaf, part of an expedition of Irish women and men who landed in the Hayle estuary. Most of her companions were massacred, including their leader Gwinear, and the bodies were left lying in a field, until the beheaded Gwinear appeared in a dream to a local Cornishman and asked him to bury them. Ia was one who survived and her mission is remembered at St Ives.

Piran's method of transport was traditionally a millstone. Like many others, he crossed from Wales to Cornwall and over to Brittany. At Perranzabuloe, on the north coast of Cornwall, his ancient oratory lies buried under the sands, and he gave his name to the white-on-black St Piran's Cross, the flag of modern Cornwall. Brannoc is said to have made the voyage round Land's End to north Devon in a stone coffin. He was guided to his hermitage at Braunton by a white sow with a litter of piglets. Attempts have been made to explain these traditions as the leaf-shaped curragh, the use of stone as ballast, or portable altars. The greater truth lies in the willingness of these women and men to leave their country for an unknown destination and live out the life of faith wherever they landed.

One name recurs. Brychan was said to be the king who gave his name to Brecon in Wales. He is credited with an enormous family, ranging from 13 to 28 sons and 25 to 37 daughters. Almost all left home for the 'desert', and energetically set about founding churches in other Celtic lands. Whether Brychan was their biological or spiritual father, he was clearly the source of an inspirational tradition of service overseas.

Few of these saints were missionaries in the conventional sense. Some were on a personal quest to seek solitude with God. That their manifest holiness attracted other people to embrace the Christian life was a by-product. Migrations of secular Celts were also taking place on a large scale. The Irish moved into coastal areas like south-west Wales. Irish Scots migrated to the Hebrides and the nearby coast.

Thousands of Britons crossed the Channel to Brittany, fleeing the advance of the English, the pressure of refugees at home, or the yellow plague which ravaged the British Isles around 550, causing the death of Finnian of Clonard among many others. Where the Celtic people went, the Celtic Church was called to serve them.

## Samson's Pilgrimage

When Samson left Caldey Island, he went to Ireland, returning to Britain the proud possessor of a chariot. He was called to be a bishop around 540. He went to say farewell to his family and found his younger sister, who alone had not entered the monastic life, living in adultery. When she proved unrepentant, he excommunicated her. Then he left Wales.

Like many others, he sailed first to Cornwall. Here, he hired a cart for his baggage, communion vessels and books, and horses for his Irish chariot. At Trigg, he ran into a pagan festival: on a hilltop was a standing stone and an idol, before which old mysteries were being enacted. When Samson told them that this was no way for Christians to behave, there was an angry scene, with the Cornish asserting their right to celebrate as their ancestors had. A ritual horse-race began and a lad was thrown in front of Samson. He lay paralysed, his neck twisted. Samson's prayer restored him to his weeping kin, and the chief ordered the idol to be destroyed. Samson took an iron tool and carved a cross on the standing stone. His biographer claims to have visited it and traced that mark with his own hand.

Samson moved south to Fowey. Already over 60, he set sail from there for Brittany with a large company. The ships left the estuary in 'a great fleet like a flight of birds'.

The Cornish King Mark had put the rightful king of Brittany to death. The young heir Judual fled to Paris, only to be imprisoned by the Frankish King Childebert. Having founded his first Breton monastery at Dol, Samson decided to get involved in politics, and set off for Paris to win the boy's release. When his request was refused, he cursed the king's descendants. Childebert changed his mind, but his queen was now Samson's implacable enemy. She tried to poison him, provided an unbroken horse with a wicked temper for him to ride, and had a fierce lion loosed in his path – but Samson confounded all her plots with the sign of the cross or a pursuing curse. After 12 years he pleased the king by getting rid of a marauding serpent: Samson tied his stole round its neck and coaxed it to the other side of the Seine. He got what he wanted at last, and sailed back to Brittany, bringing prince Judual to claim his kingdom.

Childebert gave him land around Rouen to found more monasteries. One of these, the Pental, was a refuge for penitents. It was surrounded by marshes, alive with thousands of geese and ducks. After it had rained, the wildfowl used to make so much noise that the monks could hardly hear themselves pray or sing. Finally, Samson marched out and ordered them to be quiet: 'Now, get into the monastery without a sound.' The geese and ducks fell into line and marched in through the gate. They remained all night in crestfallen silence. At dawn he released them, on their promise not to offend again, and with a last cry they took flight and disappeared over the horizon.

The disconcerting thing is that these stories, including three about dragons, were written within 50 years of Samson's death by a biographer who knew him and took trouble to check witnesses. Yet through the embroidery, we catch clues to political questions on which the Church considered that it had the right to adjudicate. We get a vivid glimpse of the physical reality of a marshland 'desert'. There is also the standard theme of the wicked queen who prevents her husband from aiding the saint. Those of us who are enthusiasts for Celtic Christianity celebrate, rightly, the role of its women – but interwoven with this is a strand of misogyny.

The monastic movement sweeping the Celtic lands had not taken the same hold on the Continent. Their churches remained pre-eminently non-monastic and diocesan. There was now a Frankish archbishop in Tours, where Martin had once been hauled from his hermit's hut; the immigrant Celts of Brittany did not accept his authority over them. Irish and, to some extent, British abbeys no longer regarded bishops as having their old importance. The relationship of the Church in Brittany with that in the rest of France was an uneasy one. They sent representatives to councils in Paris, but then carried on in their own way.

Samson conducted missions to Jersey and Guernsey, and probably reached the Scilly Isles. He returned to Dol and died there around 563, aged 80. In the abbey church his followers kept his two staves, a jewelled episcopal crozier and a sturdy walking staff. Leaders like Samson played two roles: they were ecclesiastical princes, people who could do God's business with kings and represent the people, and also rugged pilgrims, working like peasants and walking the hard road.

## Gildas's Pilgrimage

Gildas, Samson's contemporary, is remembered in many places. He probably wrote *The Ruin of Britain* on the island of Flatholm in the Bristol Channel. There is a tradition that he fasted at Glastonbury, clad in goat hair. The Irish Church honoured him for a visit in which he gave them their liturgy. For all his criticism of the egalitarian David, the Bretons remember Gildas as a social reformer. They say that he insisted that the Irish monasteries recruit from the poor as well as the nobility, and on freeing those 'enslaved by tyrants', which probably means captured slaves. This upper-class liberalism is certainly typical of Pelagianism.

Brittany also claims Gildas's death. His last request was that his body be put into a boat and set adrift. Perhaps he dreamed of being washed up on Brendan's Island of Promise. But crowds put out to sea in pursuit. Before they could reach the coracle, a wave capsized it, and Gildas's corpse sank beyond the reach of relic hunters.

# Paul Aurelian

The year 540 marks a significant tidemark in the recognition of the monasteries by the rest of the British Church. It was then, or shortly before, that Gildas produced *The Ruin of Britain*, damning the secular, worldly Church. It was probably about then that Samson, once regarded as an eccentric extremist even by his own monks, was acclaimed bishop by the Church, and the monk Paul Aurelian was summoned from Wales to be made bishop to the Cornish. Many Celtic saints may have wanted to turn their back on the sinful world, but the world beyond the monastery gates had decided that it needed them.

Paul Aurelian was yet another of that inspired generation of Illtyd's students at Llantwit. He was invited to the court at Castle Dore, above Fowey, where, like Samson, he fell out with King Mark. Allegedly, Paul asked for one of seven bells with which the king summoned his court to dinner, and Mark refused to give it. Whatever the real nature of the demand, Paul expected a different relationship between court and Church. He left in anger.

He crossed to Brittany, founded monasteries and left his name in the city of St Pol-de-Leon. Hundreds of others like him found their way to Brittany. Besides the great monastic founders, there were solitaries who set up hermitages, first by the sea-shore, then in the forest. Before the coming of these British migrants, Brittany was sparsely populated. Hermits often found themselves appealed to by refugee Britons lacking a pastor. Without support from an abbot or diocesan bishop, they set about serving this spontaneous parish. Many saints still honoured in France are Britons whose names have long been forgotten in their native country.

# White Martyrdom

Others reached Celtic Galicia in northern Spain. Some sailed into the unknown north, to the Shetland Islands, Orkney, the Faroes. When the Norwegians invaded Iceland in the ninth century, they were told Celtic *papas* had been there before them, and were shown their books, handbells and staffs. The sea was to these sailor monks what the desert had been to the first Egyptian monks. They chose islands for their hermitages.

Some did actively evangelize, especially in country areas which had remained largely untouched by the urban-based Roman churches. Others saw a duty to move as their tribe moved. It is hard to resist the feeling that some were simply seized with a spirit of adventure that needed some challenge to replace the cattle raids of their bloodier past. Many went seeking God on an entirely personal spiritual quest.

Celtic pilgrimage is a journey of faith, a one-way ticket to a destination of God's choosing. In pilgrimage, says the *Old Irish Life of St Columba*, we are 'seeking the place of our resurrection.'

Such a journey involves risk and sacrifice. One of the oldest Irish texts we possess offers us three categories of martyrdom: white martyrdom, when we abandon everything we love for the sake of God, though it costs us fasting and toil; green martyrdom, when we abandon desire itself; red martyrdom, when we are crucified or destroyed for Christ's sake. At the end of this sixth century, the Irish monk Columban travelled across Europe. He was forced out of one place after another, yet refused to be deported back to Ireland. When asked what vision drove him to wander on over half a continent, he answered, 'The salvation of many, and a solitary spot of my own.'

It is hard to better that.

# 10
# *Iona*

## *Kentigern*

Journeys made within the British Isles were no less transforming than those made overseas. We have no early *Life* of Kentigern. He comes to us on a wave of colourful stories, similar to those in many saints' *Lives*. There is the father who tries to destroy mother and baby. Kentigern is said to have been the result of rape by Prince Owain, son of the British King Urien of Rheged. In reality, Kentigern was born much earlier, probably around 518. Kentigern's pregnant mother, Thanau, princess of Lothian, either could not or would not name the father. The legend says that she was thrown over the sheer drop of Traprain Law. When she miraculously survived this, she was cast adrift on the Firth of Forth in a coracle without oars. She was washed ashore at night and staggered to the remains of a shepherds' camp-fire. There she gave birth to a son. The shepherds found them in the morning and took them to Serf, another graduate of Whithorn. The saint baptized the boy Kentigern, but he is remembered in the dedication of churches in Scotland as Mungo, 'Dear Fellow', Serf's affectionate nickname for him. The boy grew up in Serf's school, with his master's pet robin.

He completed his monastic training with Fergus of Carnach. True to another familiar theme, when his abbot died around 550, Kentigern is said to have put the body on a cart drawn by two wild bulls, and he and his companions followed where the beasts led. When they reached a cemetery associated with Ninian, the bulls refused to go any further.

Here, Kentigern planted his new settlement, which became known as Glasgow, the 'Happy Family'.

The themes of the endangered baby and the animal guide were familiar in Celtic mythology. Within the Christian tradition, they represent the word of God which cannot be stifled, and the journey undertaken at the leading of the Spirit.

Ninian had journeyed north from Whithorn bringing the Gospel to the Southern Picts. Kentigern was now able to work from a more northerly base. How far his travels took him, it is difficult to be sure. A later age recalled with surprise how he had dressed in the roughest goat hair and carried a staff not gilded and studded with jewels, but of plain wood. When his monks had 'reached maturity in age and doctrine', they lived alone. He had a reputation for well-chosen speech, 'flavoured with salt, adapted to every age and sex'. Yet the saint preached 'more by his silence than many scholars and kings do by shouting'. He was a robust, cheerful man, strong enough to stand great fatigue.

A new king, Morcant, seized control of the region and Kentigern fell out with him. His permission to operate in the north was withdrawn and he went into exile. He is said to have found eventual sanctuary in south-west Wales, at David's monastery of Menevia, but his energy and ability could not be satisfied there. He moved on to a site in north Wales, on the River Clwyd. It must have seemed as though his mission to the Picts was over.

Across the sea to the north of Wales lay Whithorn, source of Britain's monastic inspiration. As the English swept eastwards, the White House went up in flames. Its library, that granary of Greek and Latin learning and the work of generations of scholar monks, burned. There must have been grief throughout the Celtic Christian world. Those were the books which had inspired the great schools of Wales and Ireland. They survived now only in the copies its students had taken with them.

# Ciaran

Many of Whithorn's students had found their way to Clonard, foremost among the new monastic colleges of Ireland. Here, Finnian welcomed students from far afield, as Whithorn had welcomed him. Ciaran was one of the most gifted. He was possibly a Pict and certainly not an aristocrat – he is said to have been the son of a craftsman, a maker of chariots. His biographers proudly refer to him as 'Ciaran, son of the craftsman', and also a son of 'the Craftsman who made heaven and earth'. This was clearly a shaft aimed at the aristocratic abbots.

When a new student arrived to find all the available books taken, he was told to see if any of the others could lend him one. They all refused except Ciaran, who handed over the copy he was reading. Next day, in front of his jubilant classmates, the brilliant Ciaran was obliged to explain why he had only learned half the work set. They nicknamed him 'Half-Matthew'.

Ciaran had come to Finnian from Enda's strict school on the Aran Islands. At Clonard, he was embarrassed when Finnian asked him to take care of a girl student, a princess, 'just until we can build a house for the girls'. As he helped her study the Psalms he kept his eyes down, so that he never saw anything of her but her feet. The hostel was built, and Finnian's mother and sister took over as wardens.

The experience did not deter Ciaran from co-education. At a very young age, he founded his own monastery at Clonmacnois on a bend of the Shannon River in central Ireland. He had a dormitory for the girls. In time, there was opposition to this practice from more extreme ascetics, but the greatest scholar-teachers supported it. Girls continued to study at Clonmacnois, where Hebrew, as well as Greek and Latin, was taught. A miller's daughter was desperate to marry Ciaran, but he persuaded her to join his community instead, bringing others from her household. There are several stories of Ciaran begging freedom for slave-girls, who then came to Clonmacnois.

Ciaran died at 33. Columba, his contemporary, is said to

have remarked jealously, 'If he'd lived to be an old man, he'd have made more enemies.' There was a story that Ciaran had a dream in which the angels heaped more honours on Columba than on him. When he complained that this was not fair, he was told that Columba, a prince, had sacrificed more for God than Ciaran, the son of an artisan. Such stories may reflect later rivalries among abbeys, but there may well have been personal conflict between the two men.

## Columba

Do not be misled by Columba's name. As a boy he was so often in and out of the little oratory that he was nicknamed Colum-cille, 'the Dove of the Church'. But he had another name: Crimthann, 'the Fox'. There are beautiful stories about his later life, like his hospitality to a crane exhausted after a flight from Ireland. But Columba is not a man to get sentimental about. He was a tall, strong figure, with a powerful voice and a fierce temper.

He was born in Donegal in about 521 into the royal family of the northern Ui-Neill. The chieftainship did not pass automatically to the eldest son: the best man or woman was chosen from a pool of eligible candidates of the blood royal. Given his descent, organizing ability and strong personality, Columba would have been well qualified for the job. He chose instead to become a monk. At 19 he went to Moville, where the abbot was another Finnian, also a graduate of Whithorn. He learned Irish poetry and music from the bard Gemman. Finally, in his thirties, he joined Finnian of Clonard, in that remarkable generation which included Ciaran, Brendan the Navigator and Comgall, who went on to found the abbey college of Bangor on the Ulster coast.

Columba had already left Clonard before the yellow plague in the late 540s which claimed its founder. He had begun founding monasteries himself, the typical aristocratic abbot. Durrow and Kells became famous for their splendid manuscripts, but Columba's first and favourite was Derry, the 'Place of Oaks'.

Like many of his generation of Irish abbots, he never became a bishop. There is a story that Finnian of Clonard sent him to be consecrated. The officiating bishop was busy in the fields and, in a fit of absentmindedness, he only ordained Columba a priest. Columba accepted this as the will of God and kept this status for the rest of his life. In the Celtic Church he did not need to be a bishop. His power came through the monasteries he founded on both sides of the Irish Sea.

He left Ireland when he was in his early forties. The traditional story is the first recorded action for breach of copyright. His old teacher, Finnian of Moville, came back from Rome with a new book, probably the Psalter in Jerome's Latin translation. The Celtic churches had a passionate enthusiasm for the Psalms, only rivalled by their love of the Gospel of St John. Columba longed for his own copy. Finnian either refused him permission to make a transcript or indicated that it would be a waste of time asking. Columba made his copy in secret. It was a considerable labour to copy out 150 psalms by hand. Doing it stealthily at night would be risky, with monks rising for worship every three hours. Perhaps the trusting Finnian lent him the book outside the monastery.

Columba took what he wanted, but a treasure like that could not remain secret for long. When Finnian found out, he insisted that Columba's copy belonged to him, as owner of the original. Columba refused to give it up and the case went to the High King Diarmait at Tara. He was of the southern Ui-Neill, rivals to Columba's northern branch. Diarmait's verdict was, 'To every cow belongs its calf'. Columba was ordered to hand over the work to Finnian.

He refused, and stormed back to his royal kin in a towering temper. There was more than a book behind this: tales of enmity between the Ulstermen of the north and the rest of Ireland went right back into mythology. There was also a more recent quarrel. Diarmait had violated the sanctuary of one of Columba's churches to seize a murderer. Columba was not going to let Diarmait win this time.

The result was the Battle of Culdrevny. Long afterwards,

the *Cathach*, or 'Battler', was carried round the Ulster army before warfare, to bring victory. It is a Psalter in a jewelled case, said to have belonged to Columba. It looks as if it had been written in a hurry. Columba's side won this bloody battle, but thousands lay dead.

The Church was appalled. Columba was sentenced to excommunication. It was a dangerous moment, for him and for society. Columba was a powerful figure, politically and ecclesiastically, with a considerable following: he might not have gone quietly. The intervention of two senior figures saved the situation. One was another Brendan, abbot of Birr; the other, extraordinarily, was Finnian of Moville, who interceded for the former pupil he believed had cheated him. Columba's soul friend Laisren, from the hermitage of an island in Lough Erne, set an alternative penance. Columba was to be exiled from Ireland, to redeem as many souls as the number of deaths he had caused.

## *The Founding of Iona*

The year was 563. Columba set sail with the traditional number of 12 companions, bound for 'Alba of the Ravens', north Britain. Tradition says that he landed several times, but always the mountains of home were in sight. At last his coracle grounded in a cove of the small Hebridean island of Iona. From its highest hill he could no longer glimpse his beloved Ireland. He did not expect to return.

This tradition may or may not be entirely true. Yet it is startling to read, even in a *Life* based on sources close to Columba's time, that this remarkable saint was excommunicated. Modern biographies cut heroes down to size. Writers seize on any hint of scandal in their subject's life. But hagiographers were expected to pile on miracles and good deeds. An event as shocking as excommunication, even though the writer supplies a vision of angels which persuades Brendan to overturn it, sounds convincing because of its sheer unexpectedness.

The most important truth of the story is its twin concepts

88

of penance and pilgrimage. The sinner was expected to share something of Christ's suffering. The Celtic vision of pilgrimage was a journey for life.

In fact, Columba did return to Ireland at least twice, and played a part in its councils. He remained a prince and a politician, as well as a church leader. This means that Columba's choice of Iona may have been made before he set out. He and his companions were not going into virgin territory. West Argyll had recently been colonized by Scots, people from Ireland who had set up a coastal kingdom to which they brought the Irish name of Dalriada. It was land gained from the Picts, with whom the Scots had an uneasy truce. Columba went there to serve as Christ's presence to his kindred, and to continue his part in court politics.

Iona is a small island beyond the much larger island of Mull, which lies between it and the mainland. Yet it would be a mistake to think of it as remote and unexplored. Already it was the burial place of kings and, 13 years before Columba landed, the monk Oran had died there.

Columba's monks made their settlement on the east shore, beside the narrow strait to Mull. They built individual huts, probably of wood and wattle on a stone base. There were some trees, as well as rocks, gorse and heather, with a huge meadow on the western shore, but his biographer tells of oak timbers having to be towed across for the church. Columba's cell was on a knob of rock higher than the rest, and he slept on a slab of stone, with another stone for a pillow. Before long, the abbey had the usual small church, refectory and kitchen, library, scriptorium and guest-house, surrounded by an earth bank, as well as a smithy, kiln, mill and barns. There was a fleet of small boats, and visitors who wanted to be ferried over hailed the abbey from across the sound. Columba allowed no women in his monastery, but there were Columban nunneries just across the water, on other islands or on the coast.

As the numbers grew, the community was divided into Seniors, Workers and Juniors. The Juniors, who had not yet taken their vows, studied and helped with practical tasks.

The Workers were farmers and fishermen, as well as teachers; they hunted for seals, which provided fur for cold-weather bedcovers. The Seniors copied manuscripts and conducted worship. Saturday, as in Jesus's time, was a day of rest. Sunday was the peak day for services, with the weekly celebration of the Eucharist.

The sea was a high road, not a barrier. It could be dangerous, with monks in peril from the whirlpool of Corryvrechan – but so was travel by land. The king of Dalriada held his principal court at Dunadd, overlooking the Sound of Jura, gateway to the Hebrides. Columba's influence at this court was strong.

## Mission to the Picts

Columba was in a more delicate position with the older inhabitants of this land. The Picts had not surrendered their claim to overlordship of the Argyll coast and the Hebrides. Iona was still disputed territory. The Pictish King Brude ruled from his fortress of Inverness across the mountains, at the eastern end of the Great Glen. Columba needed to win him over for political as well as missionary motives. A year after his arrival, he set out for Inverness with colleagues who spoke the Pictish language.

The Great Glen is a deep trough cutting through Drum Alban, the 'Spine of Britain'. It is threaded by a chain of lochs, the deepest of which is Loch Ness. We are told that when Columba's party came to the shore, the boat was on the other side. Local people warned them of an underwater monster which had seized and half-eaten a swimmer, whom they were burying even now. Undeterred, Columba ordered a monk to swim for the ferry. Lugne had reached midstream when the monster roared up from the depths, its mouth wide open. Everyone else was struck dumb with terror, but Columba made the sign of the cross and thundered, 'Don't touch him! Get back where you came from, and be quick about it!' Still the monster came on until, only a spear's length from the desperately swimming Lugne, it turned and fled 'as if it had been towed away by ropes'.

Columba's arrival at Brude's court was resisted by his druids, who had most to lose. There are stories of contests with the chief druid, Broichan. The door of the royal fortress was shut against Columba, but flew open at the sign of the cross and the saint's knock. The druids tried to drown out the Christians' chanting, but Columba's voice proved more powerful. Columba threatened Broichan with death unless he released a Scottish woman he was holding as a slave; then, when Broichan was choking for breath, Columba cured him and the slave gained her freedom.

These stories suggest protracted opposition, but King Brude was finally won over. Columba's Church had permission to preach to the Picts, taking Irish Christianity across the highlands and islands. Brude confirmed the gift of Iona, giving Columba the backing of the Picts, as well as the support of the Scottish king of Dalriada.

## Kentigern Returns

Further south, things had changed. In 573, rival Celtic kings clashed in the battle of Arderydd near Carlisle, a slaughter so dreadful that it was said to have driven Merlin insane. Rhydderch the Generous took over Morcant's kingdom of Strathclyde, and invited Kentigern back. Kentigern, we are told, left his Welsh monastery to his kinsman Asaph, after whom the site is now named. Then he left by the north door of the church, with a procession of monks. After they had gone, this door was never opened, except on St Asaph's day.

Kentigern was met by King Rhydderch, who took him for his soul friend, placing his secular authority under him. Kentigern set up a new base at Hoddam, north of the Solway Firth, then took up his interrupted mission from Glasgow. Educated monks and practical lay workers went out in all directions. The extent of Kentigern's own travels is hard to judge. But the *papas* who eventually reached the distant islands of Papa Westray in the Orkneys and Papa Stour in the Shetlands were probably successors of his British mission. Columba's Irish monks would have used the word *ab* for 'father'.

Columba had gone beyond being Christ's servant to his own people. His Irish Church had secured a base from which to work among the Picts. There is a tradition that he was not pleased to find Kentigern conducting a similar mission from the south.

## Church and Politics

In 574, King Conall of Dalriada was killed by the Picts. It was Columba who decided the succession. He had intended to inaugurate one of Conall's older sons, but felt prompted by the Spirit to choose the much younger Aedan. The inauguration ceremony Columba conducted on Iona is said to have been the first in which the monarch was anointed with holy oil.

A year later, Columba accompanied Aedan to Ireland for the Council of Drumceatt. One issue was of particular concern to him. It was the Celtic custom to maintain the bards at public expense. Their numbers had grown, although their function as cultural guardians was being taken over by the abbeys. A proposal was made to abolish their privileges. Columba, a trained and practising poet, spoke up in defence of the bards, on condition that they lowered their demands and attended to their task of teaching. He won the day, and 1200 bards sang a paean of praise in his honour. It was said that Columba was so proud of this that a friend had to draw his attention to the fact that the sky above him was full of sniggering demons.

In 580 Aedan carried out a terrible raid on the Orkneys. There is a tradition that Kentigern's mission had already reached that far, and that he pleaded with Brude to protect the people. The Pictish king asserted his right as overlord and drew a line between the spheres of influence he allowed to Kentigern's British Strathclyde and Columba's Scottish Dalriada. The stories of Kentigern are late and unreliable, and no *Life* of Columba mentions him. Still, we are given a splendid picture of their reconciliation in 584: the church leaders processed towards each other, preceded by choirs singing different psalms. In token of their territorial stand-off, there was an exchange of staffs. Then they returned to Iona and Glasgow.

Clearly, then or later, Columba's and Kentigern's Churches were rivals. Whoever told that story wanted to knock their heads together and sit them down at the peace table. Today, the Iona Community has bases at Iona and Glasgow, uniting spirituality with social concern.

In contrast to this rivalry, another story says that, a year before this meeting, an Irish bishop came over to anoint Kentigern bishop of Glasgow, 'in accordance with British and Irish custom'. But, of course, it might have been a bishop from the south of Ireland.

## *Church and People*

Columba also refused to hear the confession of Donnan, leader of an independent Irish community on Eigg. The reason given is modesty, because Columba could foresee Donnan's martyrdom in an early Viking massacre; but it may actually have been jealousy for Iona.

There are mellower stories. Columba's monks loved him. When the work got too heavy, they felt his spirit taking their burden on himself.

The Columban Church served the secular community too. They gave the wealth they received to the poor, and bargained for the freedom of slaves. A woman told Columba that she could not bear physical relations with her husband and wanted to leave him to join a community of nuns. Instead of applauding this, Columba reconciled her to her husband and their love was stronger than before.

The style of Celtic mission was not that of the evangelistic rally. We do not read of mass baptisms. These saints went out across whatever country they settled in, taking the Gospel. But their principal concern was to be the presence of the Church wherever they were. Their evident holiness impressed witnesses. People saw that the Church cared for them. It spread by attracting people to it, rather than by going out and getting hold of them. This strength of conviction stood throughout the bad times, when mass conversions of other missions fell away.

In spite of (or perhaps because of) the strictness of their discipline, the monks and nuns gathered a large following. More recruits kept arriving on Iona, from Britain as well as Ireland. There were even two Englishmen. Other monasteries, for men and for women, followed. Tiree became the island where serious sinners were sent to serve penance.

## Death of Columba and Kentigern

Columba and Kentigern both worked until the end of their long lives. Columba's penance proved a one-way voyage in the one sense that really mattered. In May 597, in his seventies and in failing health, he asked to be taken in a chariot round the island so that he could bless the work. A month later, with his attendant Diormit, he managed to walk as far as the abbey barn, and gave thanks to find it full of corn. On the way back he was overcome with weariness and sat down at the roadside. The white pack-horse, which hauled the milk from the cowshed, came up and nuzzled its head into Columba's breast, crying with sorrow. When Diormit tried to drive it away, Columba told him, 'Leave him alone; he loves me.' These two old friends took farewell of each other.

Columba climbed a little knoll overlooking the abbey, and blessed Iona's future. Then he went back to his hut and resumed copying Psalm 34. He got as far as, 'Those who seek the Lord do not lack any good thing.' With his last strength he managed a footnote: 'I must stop here. Let Baithene write what comes next.'

He was still alive when night fell. Lying in his cell, he committed the good of the monastery to his monks and they left him resting. The bell rang for the midnight service, the Lord's Day. A final burst of energy sent Columba running into the church ahead of all the others. Diormit rushed out after him. For one glorious moment he saw the whole church lit up from within. Then, darkness. Stumbling through the shadows, he found his abbot lying in front of the altar. The rest came hurrying in with lights and Diormit lifted Columba's hand in a mute blessing. He died without speaking.

Kentigern outlived Columba by six years. He was now in his eighties and his jaw had become so slack he was afraid his gaping mouth would distress the brothers. He had it bound in place with a bandage, restoring its resolution and permitting him to speak. It is said that he died on 13 January, around 603. This would be Epiphany by the old calendar, and the writer draws attention to the large numbers traditionally baptized at this festival. There is a curious story that Kentigern died in a warm bath, which he had first blessed with the sign of salvation, and with a circle of the brothers standing around. It sounds as though he was in the act of administering the sacrament of baptism.

Columba was not the first Christian among the Scots and Picts, but the Church he established on Iona became revered far beyond that little Hebridean island. As the wave of Columban Christianity rolled south, it met another tide coming north. The year of Columba's death, 597, saw a new mission arrive in the farthest south-east corner of Britain.

# 11

## *Europe*

### *Columban*

In 559, Columba's friend Comgall founded one of many abbey colleges called Bangor. His was on the north-east coast of Ulster. To join him came a young monk whose Irish name was Colum, and who also signed himself in Latin as Columba, 'the Dove'. To distinguish him from the earlier Columba or Colum-cille, 20 years his senior, he is known as Columban or Columbanus. He was no more peaceable a man than his older namesake: he is usually, and more appropriately, pictured with a bear.

Columban had a protective mother, who would let no one but herself care for the infant. Reluctantly she released him to the monks' school. As he became a tall teenager, his good looks attracted the attention of the local girls. Columban, schooled in the ascetic view of life, was horrified by the emotions he was experiencing. He appealed to a hermit, and she confirmed that he should flee temptation. She herself had left her father's house and, had she not been a woman, she would have taken the pilgrim way across the water. Columban rushed home and declared his intention. When his frantic mother threw herself on the doorstep to stop him, he jumped over her in his haste to get away.

In reality, he served a long apprenticeship before he was ready to go abroad. First he went to Laisrenn's island monastery on Lough Erne, then on to Comgall's new abbey, Bangor. In 590, already about 50, Columban was still a monk under Abbot Comgall. Yet he took the initiative. He asked his abbot for permission to set out for continental Europe. It is typical of Celtic pilgrims that, penances apart, they did not undertake these journeys at the orders of a superior but from experience of a personal spiritual call. Celtic monks exercised a greater freedom of action than was possible under Benedict's Rule, increasingly adopted by Continental monasteries.

Columban did, however, need the permission of his abbot, and Comgall was reluctant to grant it. He had himself felt the desire to take to the pilgrim road in his youth, but had seen it as a temptation away from his real work in Ireland. In the end he relented. Columban set out with a band of companions, including his friend Gall.

## Burgundy

They landed in Brittany, picked up more recruits and made their way across a Europe racked by heathen invasions from the north, and violent feuds among the Frankish ruling family which had carved up Gaul. They reached the troubled land of Burgundy, where King Guntram made them welcome and offered them a site in the Vosges mountains. Guntram was known as 'the Good'. In this family, the term was relative. He was thought to be responsible for only two murders.

The monks settled in the Roman ruins of Annegray, surrounded by foothills which had reverted to forest. The first year was perilous. They were not yet self-sufficient in food and they nearly starved. Then a desperate farmer came to the gates, with his horses loaded with bread and vegetables, begging them to pray for his sick wife. When she recovered, they were inundated with offers of help, and the resolute holiness of their lifestyle began to attract crowds of followers.

The secular Church in Burgundy had gone the way of the British Church which Gildas had condemned so colourfully in *The Ruin of Britain*. It did uphold the Christian traditions of feeding the poor and freeing slaves, but Church appointments, including that of bishop, could be bought. The Frankish aristocratic rulers were corrupt, and the Church was too dependent on the secular state and too accustomed to seeing luxury and vice among its own clergy to oppose them effectively. There were monasteries in Gaul, but the rush to this alternative morality had not reached the extremes it had in the British Isles. The Burgundian people saw something in these Irish ascetics which was new and powerfully appealing.

Recruits flocked in. Soon it became necessary to found a larger monastery at Luxeuil, where the warm springs had once been the site of a Roman spa. And then even that needed an overflow, at Fontaines. There were also monasteries for women, whose numbers required more oratories to be built to contain them all. The nuns outside Luxeuil were famous as beekeepers.

Here Columban began to develop his Rule, based on the rigorous asceticism he had learned at Bangor. Corporal punishment was freely handed out, even for trivial faults. Coughing before the psalms could bring six lashes of the cane. The maximum for any offence was 50 lashes, not more than 25 to be administered at one time. The normal diet was bread and vegetables, though fish was also eaten and beer provided. But for the violent lay society around him, Columban's penitential code brought a new set of values. The punishment for murder, for example, was to go unarmed into exile for three years and then return to do the work the victim would have done for his parents. Paying for medical care and working for the victim were also required from anyone who caused injury. There were also lighter touches within the monastery: we read, for instance, of a bowl of roses in the classroom. Columban had inherited the Irish tradition of a liberal education. He wrote poetry and admired the Greek poet Sappho. He advised his pupils to study her style when writing their own verses, as he did.

Benedict had drawn up his Rule some 60 years earlier. Against the violent background of sixth-century Italy, it reads like a model of moderation. Individual ascetics still chose to go beyond the basic requirements, but the atmosphere was far removed from Columba's stone bed and

Samson sleeping on his feet. Quilts and pillows were allowed to the Benedictine monks; their food was nourishing, with two cooked dishes a day and a pint of wine. Punishment for sins was less severe than under Columban's Rule, often being limited to temporary loss of fellowship. Benedict's Rule placed an emphasis on stability in one place which was foreign to the restless Celtic tradition, where monks and nuns could move around abbeys in search of learning and a closer encounter with the Spirit.

It was in the Vosges mountains that Columban met his bear. In search of solitude, he reached the foot of a precipitous cliff. High up in the rock face, he saw a dark cave which looked just the place for an Irishman to find his personal hermitage. The she-bear already in residence thought otherwise. Columban persuaded her to leave. He was a big, vigorous man, not accustomed to being intimidated by fearsome opposition.

## Celtic Easter

And opposition Columban was now meeting, from the Burgundian bishops. It had not occurred to Columban to submit himself to the Burgundian Church – their sort of diocesan organization was outside his experience. In his own eyes he was the head of an autonomous abbey and he carried on exactly as he would have done in Ireland, without asking anyone's permission and without conforming to local customs. The Burgundian Church was further startled to discover Columban's churches celebrating Easter at a different time from themselves.

A calendar for Easter had been agreed at the Council of Arles in 314, which bishops from Britain had attended. Since then, several new calculations had been drawn up, and the rest of Europe, the Eastern churches and Africa had changed their practice accordingly. Easter is the greatest feast of the Christian year: for months before and after it, other fasts and feasts depend upon its date. Yet, unlike the feast of the Nativity, the date of Easter changes each year. It is related to the Jewish feast of Passover – when the Gospels say that Christ was crucified – and that depends on the lunar calendar, being the fourteenth day after the new moon following the spring equinox. If that were all, it should still have been relatively simple – though there were differences over forecasting the equinox. But further complications had arisen. Since the resurrection took place on the first day of the week, it was decided that Easter Day must always be a Sunday – and those who refused this change were branded heretics. Some years, Easter Sunday still coincided with the feast of Passover. Objectors claimed that Christians should never celebrate at the same time as the Jews. They won, and fresh tables were drawn up, with dates calculated for decades ahead. The Celtic Churches still worshipped by the old tables. They saw nothing wrong with sharing their feast day with the Jews.

Columban's monks and nuns celebrated Easter in Burgundy as the Irish had always done, and so did the converts who flocked to their churches. It was not the only visible difference. These monks shaved their heads in the Celtic fashion, in front only, in contrast to the new European style of leaving a ring of hair around a shaved circle, representing Christ's crown of thorns. They also brought their Celtic liturgy for baptism, which differed in some particulars from the Roman rite. The Burgundian bishops expected Columban, on their territory, to conform to their rules. He thought otherwise. He continued to exercise the same freedom of action as an abbot in Ireland.

In 600, it came to a head. It was one of those years when the Celtic Easter coincided with the feast of Passover. The Burgundians condemned him 'because we are not allowed to celebrate Easter with the Jews'. Columban told them not to be ridiculous. He wrote a vigorous letter to Pope Gregory about the difference of opinion. There are respectful phrases in his introduction, but once he gets going, Columban's attitude is not one of an inferior addressing a supreme pontiff. He takes it upon himself to set Gregory straight upon the calculation of Easter. How can it be right to celebrate a 'dark Easter', on a night when the moon does not rise until after midnight? How can a man as wise as Gregory disagree with the opinion of the great Jerome? Columban sees himself, not as a nonconformist provincial, but as guardian of the historic truth of the Church.

## Gregory

We do not know Gregory's answer. Columban blamed the Devil for the non-arrival of two letters from him. Columban had originally dreamed of reaching Rome, yet he was still in Luxeuil and regretted that physical infirmity prevented him from visiting the bishop of Rome in person.

But Gregory had a pilgrim vision of his own. He had already put into motion plans to take Roman Christianity to the British Isles. He had seen fair-haired boys, possibly slaves, and enquired where they came from. On being told they were Angles, his famous comment was, 'Not Angles but angels'. He was fired with desire to go to Britain himself and win its barbarian English conquerors for Christ. Christian pioneers frequently travelled and influenced new territories, but full-blooded missionary campaigns were not as common as the idealized *Lives* of the saints might lead us to suppose. Gregory was planning to convert a whole foreign people.

## Augustine in Kent

Gregory had wanted to go to Britain himself, but was forced by popular demand to accept the job of pope. He was now responsible not only for ecclesiastical matters, but for organizing the defences of Rome against barbarian attack. Gregory had offered the Benedictines his house on the Caelian Hill in Rome when the Lombards sacked their mother house of Monte Cassino. His choice for leader of his mission to Britain fell on the prior of this monastery. Augustine was a native of Marseilles, a very different man from the intellectual Augustine of Hippo who had clashed with Pelagius over original sin two centuries earlier. Augustine, with 40 monks, set out from Rome in the opposite direction to Columban's pilgrimage.

101

As they moved north, they heard travellers' tales about the barbarians on the edge of the known world. The monks mutinied. They sent Augustine back to Rome to plead with Gregory that it was no use: they could not speak English; they would only be killed if they went on. Gregory refused to recall them. He wrote a letter rallying their courage, cheerfully reminding them that the greater the hardship, the greater their reward in heaven, and ordering them to obey Augustine.

Early in 597, the same year as Columba's death, they reached the coast of Gaul and, with Franks as interpreters, took ship for Kent. This powerful kingdom was ruled by Aethelbert, acknowledged by other English rulers as *bretwalda*, 'Chief of Britain'. We cannot tell if the subject Britons were still keeping Christianity alive. We do know that Augustine and his monks were not the first Christians to land in Kent since the English invasion, for Aethelbert's Frankish wife Bertha was a Christian. She had arrived as a princess from Paris some 20 years earlier, bringing Liudhard as her bishop-chaplain, and she and her Frankish courtiers were worshipping in the old church of St Martin's outside Canterbury. Bertha may have been instrumental in securing Augustine's entry to Kent.

Aethelbert was initially suspicious. He ordered the newcomers into quarantine on the Isle of Thanet, 'Thunor's Island', sacred to the English thunder god. The king came to hear Augustine's message, but insisted that the meeting be in the open air. He wanted the protection of his sky god. Frightened though they may have been, Augustine's monks arrived in solemn procession, carrying a silver cross and a wooden standard painted with the figure of Christ, and chanting a litany of salvation.

The Kentish king was not converted immediately, but he gave Augustine permission to preach in Canterbury. A year later, Aethelbert accepted baptism – and many of the English followed his lead. Augustine was given freedom to renovate more of the ruined Romano-British churches of Canterbury, and he founded an abbey there. Others of his party took the message into Essex, and won its ruler too.

Augustine returned to Arles to be made archbishop of Canterbury. He worried about how to consecrate other bishops in Britain, without the normal minimum of three bishops to lay on hands. Gregory sent letters containing many patient answers to his questions. From necessity, one bishop would do to start with, but Augustine must create other bishops so that the situation would not arise in future. There should be 12 bishops subject to Canterbury, and if the mission succeeded in converting the whole island, he envisaged another archbishop for York, also with 12 bishops under him. The two metropolitans should co-operate. Seniority would rest with whoever was consecrated first. Augustine placed his first bishops in London and Rochester.

Gregory had rescinded his original, more hard-line policy, and advised that heathen temples should simply be cleansed and reconsecrated and their feast days incorporated into the Christian calendar. Augustine worried that he had seen church practices in Gaul which did not correspond to Rome's. Gregory counselled him to use his intelligence: for his church in Britain he should select the best ideas from all he had seen and bind them into one sheaf.

## *Augustine and the British Church*

Augustine knew this was not a totally heathen island, but he had grave doubts about the British Church. The differences were over practice, not theology. Information had reached Rome which made him suspect that British bishops were not always consecrated by at least three other bishops. No doubt the demotion of episcopal status with the rise of the abbeys led the Britons to place less importance on this ceremony. Tales of the unintended consecration of Brigid as a bishop, and the omission of consecration for Columba, suggest a lack of solemnity. And if there was doubt about the validity of a bishop, then the priests he ordained must be suspect too. Then there was the scandal of a different Easter, the Celtic monks' disgraceful tonsure and discrepancies in the liturgy for baptism.

103

Most serious was a fundamental difference of vision. Augustine had come specifically to convert the English. The British Christians saw it very differently. These heathen English now occupied all eastern Britain south of the Tweed, and were pushing hard for the rest. They had burned British churches, slain British priests at the altar, raped British women, and driven enormous numbers of people into the outer highland regions as refugees. The British Churches would not forgive them. They could not imagine themselves bringing these same English to salvation, as brothers and sisters in Christ. Their attitude was in marked contrast to that of the Churches of Ireland and Iona, which had never known the pain of conquest.

In 603 there was a meeting between Augustine and representatives of the British Churches. It was held in the Severn Valley, the current border between English and Britons. Augustine invited the Britons to join forces with them, but on his terms. After long argument, the British delegation objected that they could not abandon the customs of their forebears without the full consent of their people.

A larger conference was arranged. The British case was led by Dinoot, bishop-abbot of Bangor-ys-Coed in north Wales. He was backed by seven bishops, who may well have been abbots too, and many leading scholars of the Celtic Church. Before they set out, the Britons, in the Celtic Christian tradition, sought advice from a hermit. He counselled them to watch Augustine. If he rose at their approach, showing them respect as equals, they could do business with him. If he remained seated, they might as well break off negotiations.

Augustine had no doubt about his own authority. He had been sent by the bishop of Rome, and the British Church must accept his ruling. As the British contingent approached he remained in his seat. He did narrow the differences down to three demands: the British must change to the Roman calculation of Easter, they must adopt the Roman liturgy for baptism and, crucially, they must join him in his mission to convert the English.

They refused. Augustine cursed them. If they would not

104

offer eternal life to the English, then they would reap death at English hands. In fact, Augustine himself died the following year. His successor, Laurence, wrote a letter to all the Irish churches, whom he saw as part of his responsibility. He had thought that they might behave better than the British, but when the Irish bishop Dagan visited Kent, he had refused to eat with the mission to the English. Laurence had also heard about an Irish abbot in Burgundy, who seemed to be persisting in Celtic practices.

## Columban's Deportation

In 603 the Burgundian bishops summoned Columban to appear before them. He declined to come, but sent them a letter congratulating them on calling a council and advising them to do it more often.

Soon he was meeting trouble from a different quarter. His opponent now was Brunhilde, a fearsome dowager of the ruling Frankish dynasty. Her husband and son had died during bloody family feuds and she planned to rule through one of her young grandsons. She settled on the licentious Theodoric, who had inherited Burgundy. Columban berated him for his immorality and arranged a diplomatic marriage with a Visigoth princess. Brunhilde broke it up. Theodoric sent the princess back and returned to his mistresses. Brunhilde then produced two of Theodoric's illegitimate sons and demanded that Columban bless them, to underline her power. But Celtic saints were the conscience of the secular rulers, not their lackeys. Outraged, Columban castigated Brunhilde in front of the court for her family's behaviour. She decided to silence him.

The monks of Luxeuil were put under house arrest and the local populace forbidden to help them. Columban broke the ban and stormed up to the palace, but he refused to cross the threshold. When Theodoric had food sent out to him, Columban dashed the dishes on the ground. He went back to Luxeuil, but Theodoric and his companions came swaggering in. 'I've heard you have parts of this monastery forbidden to lay people.' 'It's our custom,' Columban told him. 'We have a guest-house for visitors.' 'It's not Burgundian custom,' Theodoric retorted. 'If you want to keep in with me, you're going to have to open up this place to all Christians.' He had forced his way into the monks' private quarters and Columban cursed him where he stood. Theodoric said that if he was trying to win the crown of martyrdom, he was going to be disappointed. There was another way to get rid of him.

Columban was served with a deportation order. Many of his monks swore that they would go too, but Theodoric ordered that only Irish and British monks would be allowed to accompany him. The deportees set out across Gaul, under guard. There were times on the way when the prisoners almost starved, and were only saved by the generosity of sympathisers. Their port of embarkation was Nantes. Columban was still writing to his monks in Luxeuil as the ship was weighing anchor for Ireland. 'I could escape. There's no guard around. It almost seems as if they want me to.' A skiff was to take him down the estuary, where the ship was setting sail – but before it reached the open sea, the Irish-bound vessel ran aground. The mariners decided that the rebellious monks must be the cause, and dumped them ashore. They found that the Burgundian guards had already left for home – they were free.

Back they went, right across Gaul. They avoided Theodoric's Burgundy and headed for the Alps through Austrasia, which was ruled by his brother Theodebert. Columban composed a vigorous boating song to help them up the Rhine: 'Heave, lads, and make the echoes ring.' Theodebert gave them land at Bregenz on the shore of Lake Constance, and in 612 they began monastic life again.

Here, Gall, Columban's faithful companion all this time, came into his own. They were now in reach of the German-speaking Allemani. Gall had a gift for languages and he became their principal spokesman. It nearly cost him his life. As he thundered against worship of Woden and Thunor, the Irish monks overturned idols, burned sacred trees, broke open casks of ritual beer and tumbled them into the lake.

Gall was sentenced to death for this, and Columban to a beating. They escaped just in time.

But war broke out between the ruling brothers. Theodebert's Austrasia fell to Columban's old enemies, Brunhilde and Theodoric. It was time to move on. From the outset, Columban had dreamed of reaching Rome. He decided to cross the Alps.


## Columban in Italy

When it was time to set off, Gall fell ill with fever. This was opportune for him. His skill with languages had enabled him to reach the Germanic people better than any of the others. He begged to be allowed to stay. Columban did not take kindly to being opposed. He left Gall behind but, in a parting shot, forbade him to celebrate the Eucharist as long as he, Columban, lived. Gall obeyed this. He moved on into the woods and spent the rest of his life working from the monastery now known as St Gall's. Its library has a German phrase-book almost certainly written by him.

Theodoric died suddenly and Brunhilde fell into the hands of Theodebert's party. In an execution violent even for those days, they tortured her for three days, put her naked on a camel for the sport of the soldiers and finally bound her to two wild horses which dashed her to pieces. By then, Columban was in Italy.

In 612 he was welcomed at the courts of Milan and Pavia by the Lombard King Agilulf and his influential queen Theodelinda. She was a Catholic, he an Arian, following the heresy denying the divinity of Christ which was sweeping northern Europe. But Columban was not a man for courts. In 614 they granted him land, at nearby Bobbio, for his last monastery. Columban never sought an easy life. Around the age of 70, he shouldered planks of wood with the rest, to build his new abbey.

He still could not keep out of controversy. He wrote to Pope Boniface IV about the Arian debate over the divinity of Christ which was so exercising the Church. Columban made no concession to the fact that Agilulf, an Arian, was his new benefactor. Nor did he feel inhibited from exhorting the pope to safeguard the apostolic faith or else 'lose the honour due to your apostolic office'. He considered himself qualified to be the conscience of Rome as well as the conscience of the king's court.

Columban never reached Rome. A year after Bobbio opened its gates, he died there. Back on the shores of Lake Constance, the story is that Gall, his former companion and interpreter, felt a sudden presentiment. He ordered one of his monks to make ready for him to celebrate the Eucharist. 'But you never officiate at the sacrament. Columban forbade you to do so as long as he lived,' the man replied. 'Columban is dead. I must say a mass for his soul.' A messenger was sent to Bobbio. He returned with Columban's staff, bequeathed to Gall on his deathbed as a pledge of reconciliation.

Columban said he was seeking 'the salvation of many, and a solitary spot of my own'. Others said of him, 'he hurled the fire of Christ wherever he could, no matter what a blaze it caused'.

# 12
## *Lindisfarne*

### *Aethelfrith the Ferocious*

The British and the Scots were reeling under disasters at English hands. Aethelfrith the Ferocious, warlord of Bernicia with his chief fortress at Bamburgh, killed his southern neighbour King Aelle of Deira, whose centre was York. This was the homeland of those English boys whom Gregory had seen in Rome. Aethelfrith then married Aelle's daughter Acha, and set out to exterminate her surviving male relatives. Her four-year-old brother Edwin found sanctuary on the island of Mon off the coast of Gwynedd (later named Anglesey). This little English boy, claiming descent from Woden, was fostered at a British Christian court. Cadfan must have convinced himself that 'my enemy's enemy is my friend'. Edwin grew up with Cadfan's son Cadwallon as his foster-brother.

Aethelfrith decisively defeated Aedan of Dalriada, whom Columba had anointed. In 616 he turned on the Welsh kingdoms. The British war-hosts met him near Chester, on the plain of the Dee. North Wales had several great monasteries, the foremost being Bangor-ys-Coed, 'Bangor-in-the-Wood'. These abbots saw the battle of Chester as a fight for the survival of Christian Britain, and they joined in the struggle in the way they knew best. Hundreds of monks massed on the hilltop overlooking the battlefield to curse Aethelfrith's army. Aethelfrith saw them. He believed that their invocations of his enemy's God were every bit as powerful as the spears and swords of British warriors. The monks were massacred.

Edwin, his brother-in-law, was on the run, seeking sanctuary now in English kingdoms. In Mercia, he married a princess who bore him two sons. His flight took him on to the East Anglian court. King Redwald had once visited Kent and accepted Christianity, but his strong-minded wife had other ideas. Redwald compromised. In the temple dedicated to Tiw, the red-handed god of war, and one-eyed Woden, lord of slain warriors, he installed another altar to 'the White Christ'. Edwin, brought up in Christian Wales, must have recognized it.

Aethelfrith was closing in. He first tried to bribe Redwald to hand Edwin over, then threatened him. One night Edwin's friend broke the news: Redwald was going to surrender him to the Northumbrian assassins. He must run. But Edwin had reached the end of his hope. As he sat in the darkness outside his lodging, he saw a stranger approach. The man greeted Edwin and asked what was troubling him. Edwin's first reaction was to tell him it was none of his business. The stranger persisted. What would Edwin give in return for Redwald's continued protection, the restoration of his father's kingdom, and advice that would lead to his salvation and new life? Edwin pledged everything in his power, and promised to obey the guidance of whoever could make this come true. The stranger laid his right hand on Edwin's head, telling him to remember his promise when he received that sign again. Edwin was still trying to make sense of this experience when his friend came running to tell him that Redwald had changed his mind. The queen would not hear of him sacrificing his honour and selling the life of a guest. East Anglia was going to fight Aethelfrith and restore Edwin to Northumbria.

Aethelfrith fell in the battle by the River Idle, south of the Humber. Edwin was installed as king, not just of his father's Deira, but of the northern territory of Bernicia as well. It was now the turn of Aethelfrith's children to flee into exile, escaping from Edwin as he had once fled from their father. These children's sanctuary was also a Christian island. In their case, it was Iona.

110

## Edwin's Conversion

Edwin's little great-niece Hild was born in the small Christian kingdom of Elmet, around present-day Leeds, after her exiled father had been poisoned. Now she came out of hiding, with her mother and sister. After Redwald's death, Edwin was acknowledged as *bretwalda* (head of all the English rulers) by most of the English kingdoms. It was said that during his reign a young woman with a newborn baby in her arms could walk from coast to coast without being molested. For the English, this was a statement of his power and virtue. For the British, it symbolized the extent of their loss.

Edwin raided even further west than Aethelfrith. His foster-brother Cadwallon now ruled Gwynedd in north Wales. Edwin drove him back on to Mon, which had once given him sanctuary as a boy. He chased Cadwallon out to a last refuge on the little island of Priestholm. From there, his foster-brother fled into exile, to nurse his hatred of Edwin and Northumbria.

Kent and Essex had reverted to heathen kings when their first Christian rulers died. The bishop of London fled. But soon Aethelbert's son returned Kent to Christianity. With the death of his first queen, Edwin asked the king of Kent for the hand of his sister Aethelberg. A condition of the marriage was that Aethelberg and her retinue be allowed Christian worship. Edwin further undertook to listen to her chaplain preach, and to consider conversion. Like her mother Bertha, Aethelberg was a Christian princess marrying into a heathen English court and bringing her priest with her. Paulinus had come to Canterbury with a second wave of Italian clergy, to reinforce Augustine's mission. Now he was consecrated a bishop and accompanied the new queen to Northumbria. Gregory's dream of two archbishops, at Canterbury and York, was coming closer. With them went the deacon James, famous as a musician and choirmaster.

Edwin's conversion was painful. Time and again he seemed to be on the brink, yet put off a decision. Aethelberg was pregnant with their first child. On Easter day, a visitor from the rival English kingdom of Wessex approached Edwin's chair. As he knelt to deliver his message, he suddenly jumped up and whipped out a hidden knife. Edwin's thane, Lilla, flung himself in front of his lord and died in his place. Even so, the poisoned blade pierced Edwin through his body. The shock threw Aethelberg into labour. Three lives – king, queen and baby – hung in the balance. All three were saved. The little girl, Eanfled, was born almost painlessly.

Paulinus hailed it as an Easter miracle, a sign of Christ's salvation, and called upon Edwin to respond by accepting baptism. Still the king prevaricated. As a gesture of gratitude, he allowed the baby Eanfled, accompanied by an escort of 12 Northumbrians, to be baptized. But he himself would wait until the Christian God gave him vengeance on the king of Wessex. He got that too.

He gave up going to Woden's temple. But still he agonized. Pope Boniface sent letters and gifts to him and to Aethelberg, urging him to accept salvation. Edwin went for long solitary walks, appearing deeply troubled. It was no light decision. Where the king went, his people would follow. Edwin claimed direct descent from Woden. In the English tradition, he was a priest-king, to a greater degree than were the Celtic kings. If he made the wrong choice, the English gods would be angered, and it would spell doom for the country's harvests and defeat in battle. At last, as he sat alone, someone came to him and placed his hand on Edwin's head. 'Do you remember this sign?' Edwin began to tremble and was about to throw himself at Paulinus's feet. The bishop demanded that Edwin redeem his pledge, made in East Anglia when he was at his lowest point. Paulinus may have heard this story, but it is possible that the mysterious stranger was Paulinus himself, on a visit from Kent to the lapsed Christian Redwald.

Even then, Edwin pleaded the necessity of consulting his council. Coifi, Woden's chief priest, spoke first. He might have been expected to lead the opposition to Christianity. But the aggrieved Coifi demanded, 'What have our gods done for me? I've served them all these years, yet you've abandoned their worship and bestowed your favours on other people, and what reward have I had? Nothing.' Another councillor drew their attention to a tiny sparrow, flitting into the firelit feast-hall out of the storm, only to dart out of the opposite window and be lost in rain or snow. 'Human life is like that,' he said. 'If anyone can show us a greater hope of what lies beyond, it must be better.'

Paulinus was invited to preach the call to conversion to the court. He was a tall, dark man, slightly stooped, with a hooked nose, and he could preach with charismatic eloquence. Edwin and all his Northumbrian court pledged their souls to Christ. Coifi threw off his regalia and called on the king for weapons and a stallion – both forbidden to a priest of Woden. Armed with sword and spear, and riding the king's own horse, he led a demolition squad to the sanctuary of Woden at Goodmanham. He hurled a spear into the sanctuary, ritually desecrating it – to the dismay of priests and worshippers, who thought he had gone mad. He ordered lighted brands to be flung on to the thatched roof of the temple. Goodmanham burned to the ground in a frenzy which Gregory would not have approved.

Edwin and Paulinus arranged for a small wooden church to be built quickly for his baptism in York. It was not named in the Celtic manner, after its founder, but was dedicated in the Roman way, to St Peter. On Easter eve, 627, Paulinus conducted the baptism and laid his hands on Edwin for confirmation, along with his Northumbrian court. Among those early English converts were Edwin's great-niece Hild, now a teenager, and her sister Hereswith.

All this we know from Bede's *History of the English Church and People*, carefully researched and written a century later. But Bede was an Englishman and a devoted supporter of the Roman cause. The Welsh records tell a different story.

They say that Edwin was baptized by Rhun, a British warrior prince turned priest. It is credible that the young prince Edwin, raised in Christian Wales, might have been baptized there under the influence of his foster-father King Cadfan, even if it was only as a prudent move to placate the local God. Edwin may well have abandoned his Christianity when he fled to English Mercia and married its princess. How could he confess to Paulinus and Aethelberg that he was an apostate? Would he imperil his soul by being baptized twice? He might have seized at one straw of hope: if he had heard Paulinus thunder against the irregularity of the British Church, Edwin may have seen a way out. Had Rhun been ordained by a genuinely consecrated bishop, and the baptismal service properly conducted? Was Edwin's baptism in Wales valid?

Whatever the truth behind Edwin's conversion, English Northumbrians went over to Christianity in huge numbers. Mass baptisms were held, in the River Swale at Catterick in Deira, and in the River Glen at Yeavering in Bernicia. Woden's temples were probably reconsecrated, as Gregory recommended. Excavations of the temple at royal Yeavering show that massive wooden posts were removed. One was probably the totem World Tree, on which Woden was said to have hung for nine days and nights to win wisdom. But few new churches were built in Northumbria, and Bernicia still remained largely heathen. Edwin did start the building of a larger stone church at York, enclosing the wooden one in which he was baptized. It was left unfinished when he died.

## A Place of Safety

Meanwhile, on Iona, Aethelfrith's exiled sons were growing up under the care of Columba's successors, Fergna and Segene. Acha, Edwin's sister, is said to have borne Aethelfrith six boys, of whom Oswald was the eldest, and then Oswy. There was also a baby sister, Aebbe. There was no place for her in the male community of Iona, and she may have been taken to the Isle of Women, just across the strait. These English children, claiming descent from Woden, were instructed in the Christian faith. They accepted baptism in the Celtic tradition. But the boys did not make full use of the intellectual education on Iona. Oswy, at least, remained illiterate, signing his name with a X. For the rest of their training they went to the mainland court of 'Freckled Donald' – Domnall Brecc of Dalriada – where the boys learned to be warriors. They fought in Ireland for the kindred of Domnall, Columba's family. Either then or later, Oswy had an affair with an Irish princess, Fina. Their son, Aldfrith, was in turn sent to school on Iona. Domnall Brecc wanted to marry Aethelfrith's daughter, but Aebbe refused. She had probably been educated by Celtic nuns: the possibility of a different kind of fulfilment may already have occurred to her.

The controversy between the Churches rumbled on. English Kent was now firm in its Roman Christianity. Essex was won back. In Ireland, news filtered back of changes on the Continent and Columban's difference with his neighbours. The south of Ireland exchanged much traffic with the rest of Europe and was more open to new ideas. Its churches began to go over to the new Roman ways. The north was more conservative, and so was the Iona mission, now independent of Ireland. In 633, with a mockery reminiscent of old north–south feuds, Cummian of Durrow wrote to Segene, third abbot of Iona, 'So Rome is wrong? Jerusalem is wrong? Alexandria is wrong? Antioch is wrong? The whole world is wrong. Only the Scots and the Britons have got it right!' A year later, Pope Honorius wrote to all the leaders of the Irish and Scottish Churches in the same terms. They should not think their small number 'on the furthest edge of the earth' was wiser than all the rest of Christendom. Controversy raged in Ireland, and a delegation went to Rome to sort it out. In 636, the south of Ireland decisively opted for the Roman system, but most of the north would not give in. In 640, Pope John IV was writing to complain to these abbots about their Easter observance and worrying too about a resurgence of Pelagianism. Iona would not budge on the date of Easter. If the old pattern was good enough for Columba, then it was good enough for Columba's Scottish and Pictish churches.

# East Anglia

Roman Christianity was spreading in the English kingdoms. Edwin sent Paulinus and James to the province of Lindsey, where Paulinus conducted baptisms in the Trent near Lincoln. Edwin also used his growing power to win Redwald's son, Earpwald of East Anglia, to Christianity. Earpwald was murdered by a worshipper of Woden. Three years later, his Christian brother Sigbert, who had been studying in Gaul, took over as king and Burgundy sent a missionary to the British Isles. Felix was invited to become bishop at Dunwich, under the archbishop of Canterbury.

# Defeat in Northumbria

Mercia (the English midlands) was now seized by the fearsome warlord Penda, who rapidly made it one of the most powerful English kingdoms. Penda was passionate in his defence of the old English gods, yet he formed a military alliance with the Celtic Christians of north Wales. Cadwallon, the foster-brother Edwin had driven from his homeland, had returned from exile and was now Gwynedd's king. Six years after Edwin's Roman baptism, the combined war-host of Mercia and Gwynedd marched against him.

Edwin met them at Hatfield, not far from the battlefield where his old enemy Aethelfrith had fallen. He too was killed there. One of the sons of his first marriage fell in battle; the other was captured and executed. Queen Aethelberg fled back to Kent, with the little princess Eanfled and a baby son. Paulinus packed up the church plate and fled with her. But James the deacon stayed on at Catterick for the rest of his life, teaching Gregorian chants through the good times and the bad. Hild, Edwin's great-niece stayed too.

The pope had just sent Paulinus the *pallium*, the white lamb's-wool stole embroidered by nuns in Rome, which would have made him the first archbishop of York. It arrived too late. Bede records this year as the *annus horribilis*, a year so terrible that its date should be expunged from the

116

history books. Penda split Northumbria into two again. Eanfrith, Aethelfrith's eldest son by an earlier marriage, had not stayed with the younger boys on Iona, but had been baptized and married a Pictish princess. He was allowed back as regent of Bernicia, while a cousin of Edwin's was given Deira. Penda went back to Mercia, leaving Cadwallon to wreak atrocities which did not spare women or children. Shaken by this appalling defeat, both Deira and Bernicia lapsed into the worship of their former gods. The mass conversions of Paulinus's mission were swept away as swiftly as they had happened. Then the two puppet kings made a rash bid for independence. Cadwallon slaughtered them.

## Aidan

This was the chance for Eanfrith's half-brother Oswald, raised on Iona. His friend, Domnall Brecc of Dalriada, loaned him troops – but with one injunction: they were to fight against the English only, and were forbidden to harm Cadwallon's Britons. They disobeyed that order. With these Scottish allies, Oswald and Oswy marched south, picking up Northumbrian support. Monks from Iona were probably their chaplains, praying for the war-host. They took their stand north of Hadrian's Wall, at a spot known afterwards as Heavenfield. The night before battle, Oswald had a vision. He saw Columba, so majestic that his head touched the clouds, speaking the words God had said to Joshua before he led the Israelites across the Jordan into the Promised Land: 'Be strong and courageous. I shall be with you.' Oswald raised a roughly-made wooden cross with his own hands, then called the whole army to pray. In the first light of dawn, they charged. Cadwallon was killed.

Oswald was now king of all Northumbria. In love with Celtic Christianity, he wanted his own version of Iona. His first missionary was Corman, who preached to the largely heathen Northumbrians, ranting hell-fire. But Corman found them so rough and difficult to persuade that he declared the task impossible and went home in disgust.

Back on Iona, he reported his opinion to Abbot Segene and the brothers. Visiting at the time was Aidan, a scholar bishop from the same family as Brigid. He had been at the school on Tiree in the Hebrides, and now had his own Irish abbey on Scattery Island in the River Shannon. Listening to Corman's tirade, he suggested a different approach: Iona should first offer the English the loving milk of the Gospel, before weaning them on to stronger meat. Anyone who makes a positive proposal to a committee knows what to expect. Aidan was unanimously voted the best man for the job.

At first, Aidan had to use the Irish tongue to preach to the English troops. Edwin had been a powerful king, converted to the hierarchical Church of Paulinus and Augustine. Status mattered to Edwin. Wherever he went, he had his standard, a winged sphere, paraded in front of him. King Oswald now showed Northumbria a different vision of Christianity. The king himself acted as Aidan's interpreter.

Oswald chose his own holy island. He offered Aidan Lindisfarne, within sight of the king's crag fortress at Bamburgh along the coast. Lindisfarne is a sandy outlier, cut off from the mainland at high tide. Like Iona, it fulfilled the Celtic need for solitude with God, and yet was within easy travelling distance of the court. Like Iona too, it was already the burial place of kings. It embodied both the personal and the public elements of Celtic Christianity. It was noted by a later historian that 'the Scots, who flooded into the country under the Northumbrian king's patronage, were in the habit of hiding in bogs rather than residing in fine towns'. That misses the point. A *Rule of Columcille* (though probably not the original one) required its monks and nuns to 'be alone in a secluded place, near an important centre'. They were positioned so as to be the independent conscience of the country, depending absolutely on solitude with God to give them strength for their service to the community. Aidan also made a personal retreat on the rock of Hobthrush Island, itself separated from Lindisfarne at high tide, or further out on the black ledges of the Farne Islands. The spiritual centre of Northumbria shifted from the city of York to a sandy island.

We do not hear of mass rallies, of people baptized in their thousands in Northumbrian rivers, as they had been under Paulinus's eloquence. The monks went out into the surrounding countryside. They set up the cross, preached, helped the sick. They used the wealth people gave them to feed the hungry and ransom slaves. The villagers ran out to welcome them when they saw them approaching. As so often with the Celtic missions, conversions were won more through example than exhortation. The Lindisfarne monks cared little for their own material comfort. Even their church roof leaked. Oswald often went to Lindisfarne to spend time with his soul friend. But he always left before suppertime, so that he and his men would not be a drain on the meagre housekeeping of the monks.

One of Aidan's most influential initiatives was in the true Celtic tradition. He opened a school. Twelve English boys were recruited in the first intake. They included four brothers, Cedd, Cynibil, Caelin and Chad, and another boy, Eata.

## Fursa

The Burgundian Felix was bishop in East Anglia, in the Roman tradition. But in 633 an open-ended pilgrimage brought to East Anglia the Irishman Fursa. He was both a scholar and a visionary. He saw the earth on fire with sin, and it so terrified him that the memory made him run with sweat when he was wearing a thin garment on a bitter winter's day. He founded a monastery and longed for the hermit life, but converts flocked around him. King Sigbert himself became a monk. He had to be dragged from his monastery to lead the army when Penda and the Mercians attacked, but refused to defend himself with more than a stick and was killed.

## Oswald's Death

In the same year that Fursa reached East Anglia, Birinus arrived in Wessex, commissioned directly by Pope Honorius to penetrate further into the English kingdoms. He was independent of the Canterbury mission. For him, the distinction between Roman and Celtic Churches was clearly not absolute. Birinus converted King Cynegils of Wessex, but it was Oswald of Northumbria who stood sponsor and 'lifted him out of the baptistry'.

There was an uneasy peace between Northumbria and Mercia for 12 years. Then Penda caught Oswald's depleted war-host on his western borders. Oswald fell near Oswestry, praying with his last breath for the men around him. Penda had Oswald's head and arms cut off and exhibited on stakes. Oswald's brother Oswy made a daring raid to rescue the relics. Aidan gave the head burial on Lindisfarne, while the hands and arms were enshrined in the royal church at Bamburgh. It seemed as though Celtic Christian Northumbria, and Lindisfarne, lay at the mercy of another heathen invasion.

# 13

## *Conflict*

### *Oswy and Eanfled*

Northumbria did not lapse back to the worship of its former gods with Oswald's death. Time and again, elsewhere, this was the result of defeat by Penda. But Aidan's Celtic Christianity had rooted itself in the hearts of the Northumbrian people. He had evangelized by different means from Paulinus's mass conversions. Paulinus had fled, leaving few churches and, as far as we know, only James the deacon as clergy. Aidan and his monks stayed on.

Penda split Northumbria in two again. Oswald had left a son, Oethelwald – but the boy was too young to take over. Oswy, the dead king's brother, was allowed only Bernicia. Deira went to his cousin Oswin.

Oswy's first wife was Rhiainmelt, a British princess and granddaughter to Rhun, who had given Edwin Celtic baptism. Rhiainmelt died and Oswy was free to make another political union. He chose as his second bride Eanfled, Edwin's only surviving child, who had been taken to safety in Kent.

It was a union of contrasts. Oswy represented Bernicia and the north; Eanfled, Deira and the south. As a child, Oswy had fled to Iona; as a child, Eanfled had escaped to Canterbury. He had been brought up in the Celtic Church; she in the Roman Church. Their families had attacked and killed one another. Yet they were first cousins. Their marriage symbolized the difference between the Celtic and Roman traditions. This was not a clash between two separate Churches. It was a conflict within one family.

Eanfled's grandmother Bertha had brought her chaplain to Kent, and her mother Aethelberg her's to Northumbria. Now it was Eanfled's turn to set out as a bride, bringing her Roman priest, Romanus. But there was a difference this time: Oswy was already a Christian. He sent his Celtic-trained chaplain, Utta, to escort her by sea. It was a stormy passage and Utta used oil blessed by Aidan to calm the sea. Very probably there were storms between him and Romanus as well.

The Northumbrian court was now split. Some years, the king and his retinue would be celebrating the feast of Easter while the queen and her Kentish people were still mourning Christ's passion on the cross. And this did not just affect Easter day: Lent, Palm Sunday, Ascension day and Pentecost were all out of step. For months, the king and queen kept different fasts and feasts. The monks of Lindisfarne visited the court with their Celtic tonsure – heads bare in front and with hair hanging long behind – in their unbleached white tunics. They would have been in visible contrast to Romanus's neatly clipped circle of hair and probably darker clothes. These were outward symbols of deeper attitudes. Their creeds were the same, but their outlook was different. In a society where gift-giving was practised on a huge scale, the Roman Church gave gifts to the king; the Lindisfarne monks, by contrast, gave away everything they had to the poor. The Roman mission was based at the court; Aidan, as the king's soul friend, visited the court often but maintained a spiritual distance. Roman monks were influenced by the Rule of Benedict, which stressed *gravitas*, frowning on both laughter and excess of zeal – they lived ascetic lives, but in moderation; the Celts, on the other hand, often went to extremes in their devotion. The Romans emphasized obedience to authority; the Celts celebrated their autonomy. Bede consistently praises the faithful service of Roman missionaries. Equally consistently, he tells us how the Celtic saints were loved by the people.

# Hild

Hild had conflicting loyalties. She was a great-niece of Edwin, but also of Oswald and Oswy. She had received Roman baptism under Paulinus, and now she had fallen under the spell of Aidan's Christianity. Still, there must have been times when she looked out from Bamburgh to the misty line of Lindisfarne across the water and regretted that the opportunity offered to men at its school was not open to women. She would hear from Aebbe, Oswy's sister, about the Scottish nuns in Dalriada. She knew too that, in Kent, Queen Aethelberg was now a nun with her own abbey. Kentish girls were going to Gaul to be educated. English women were founding monasteries on the Continent. Hild too longed to learn, and to teach. But there were no communities for nuns in Northumbria. Letters reached her from her sister Hereswith, once queen of East Anglia but now widowed. Hereswith had joined a double monastery at Chelles, near Paris. Hild determined to join her.

She got no further than East Anglia. While she was staying with her royal nephew, a letter from home overtook her. Aidan of Lindisfarne had recognized the need he had so long overlooked. He had given the veil to Heiu, the first English nun in Northumbria. Now he urged Hild to come back and become a nun in her native country, instead of in Gaul. She returned immediately and accepted the veil from Aidan.

Heiu was already installed as abbess at Hartlepool, on the Bernician coast. Hild founded her own community, on the north bank of the River Wear. It was a small venture, with just a handful of companions. But a year later, Heiu moved south to pioneer a new foundation. Hild took over as abbess of Hartlepool. This was a double house, for women and men. Common in the English kingdoms, such mixed communities were always headed by women. After consulting Aidan, Hild established her own Rule, bringing a more orderly regime than before.

In Hild's abbey there was no personal property. Rich and poor came to join her on the same terms. Her Rule demanded a righteous life, mercy and purity, but above all peace and love. Everyone called her Mother, and Hild became famous for her wisdom and joyful service to God. Kings and commoners came to ask her advice. Aidan and other church leaders visited her abbey to exchange ideas. There was mutual admiration and affection between her and her soul friend.

## Aidan and Oswin

There were more monasteries for men too. Eata, one of Aidan's first 12 English pupils, became abbot of Melrose, in the hill country west of Lindisfarne. A new generation of English men and women was being trained as leaders by the missionary Celts. Politically, huge tracts of Britain were now English-ruled. The balance in the Church was shifting too. When the Romans left, the Christian Celts had met the challenge to evolve their own identity. Now, it was English Christians who needed to work out for their own time what it meant to be the Church in Britain.

As well as being abbot of Lindisfarne, Aidan was bishop and pastor to all the Northumbrians. He ranged this huge territory to meet them. Whenever possible he travelled on foot, so that he could talk to everyone he met on their own level. King Oswin of Deira was his close friend. Oswin gave Aidan a horse to ride, so that he could speed on urgent journeys and cross rivers more easily. It was one of the finest animals in the royal stable, and came equipped with costly trappings. Aidan accepted it reluctantly. Soon after he set out, he met a beggar. With the same impulsive generosity as his early kinswoman Brigid, he immediately handed over the horse and its harness. When Oswin got to hear about it, he was furious: 'Why didn't you tell me you were going to give it away? I've got plenty of less valuable horses. I could have let you have one more suitable for a beggar.' Aidan rebuked him: 'What are you trying to say, sire? Is the offspring of a mare more valuable to you than a child of God?' They went in to supper and Aidan sat down, but the king stood in front of the fire, thinking this over. Suddenly he unbuckled his sword, threw himself at Aidan's feet and begged his forgiveness: 'I'll never question again what you do with my gifts.' During the meal, Aidan was seen to be weeping. When his chaplain asked him, discreetly in Irish, why, he said that he feared Oswin was too good a man to last as king. He was right.

Further north in Bernicia, Oswy resented having the Mercian king Penda as his overlord. This brought anguish to his people, with bloody punitive raids. On one occasion, Oswy and his warriors rode out against Penda, but the Mercians eluded them. When Penda's raiders reached Bamburgh, they tore the peasants' houses apart and piled the wattle walls, rafters, thatch against the walls of the royal fortress. Aidan was alone on his rock hermitage on the Farne Islands, keeping the Lent fast, when he caught sight of a pall of smoke rising from Bamburgh. Raising his hands to heaven and weeping, he prayed. The horrified monks watching from Lindisfarne saw the wind change: smoke and flames rolled back down the hill to engulf the besiegers. Bamburgh, and Oswy's family, were saved and Penda retreated for the time being.

Oswy wanted to be king of all Northumbria. He attacked his peace-loving cousin, King Oswin of Deira. Oswin rode out at the head of a war-host, but when he saw the Bernicians coming, he disbanded his troops and fled. A thane gave him hiding in a barn, but then betrayed him to Oswy. Oswin was executed.

Aidan died 11 days later, sitting under a makeshift tent against the outer wall of Bamburgh's church. The blackened post on which he is said to have been leaning can still be seen there, having survived a second attempt by Penda to torch Oswy's capital.

Aidan may have died from entirely natural causes, but it is possible to imagine what he might have been doing to fall ill outside Oswy's gate. There was an old Celtic ritual of fasting against a wrongdoer to force them to confess their crime.

## Cuthbert

Aidan's mission had borne results. Cuthbert had been brought up a Christian. As a child, he was agile and quick-witted, fond of games and pranks. The night Aidan died, the 17-year-old was watching sheep on the hills near Melrose. He had a vision of choirs of angels descending to earth to carry off a brilliant soul. When he came down to the village next day and learned of Aidan's death, he returned the sheep to their owners and announced he was going to become a monk. He came to the gates of Melrose Abbey in fine style. He had already done military service and was riding a horse, armed with a spear and accompanied by a servant. Waiting at the gate was Boisil the prior, who became Cuthbert's beloved teacher.

Cuthbert proved a good pupil and an energetic missionary. He would sometimes go out on horseback, but more often on foot. His journeys took him up into the wild hill country, to villages others feared to visit because of their barbarity and squalor. On some excursions, he was away from Melrose for as long as a month, and was often hungry on his travels. Once, a hospitable Christian woman offered him a meal, but Cuthbert was only concerned about feeding his horse. It was a Friday, so he himself would not eat until evening. The woman warned him that he might not reach his destination before sundown, and that there were no more villages on the way to give him food. Cuthbert pressed on. Overtaken by night, he took refuse in a shepherd's summer hut. The horse was all right; Cuthbert pulled straw from the roof for it. He himself went hungry. He was passing the time chanting psalms when he saw the horse reach up its neck to pull out more straw. Down tumbled a bundle containing bread and meat. Cuthbert gave half the loaf to the horse.

It was part of a pattern. He took a boy with him on one of his expeditions and they both became weak from hunger, with no shelter in sight. Then an eagle landed on the river bank and dropped a large fish. The boy ran to get it and brought it back to Cuthbert, full of pride. But the saint scolded him: 'Doesn't the servant get its share? Quick now, cut it in two and give half to the bird.' They soon came in sight of a house and shared the remainder of the fish with the family there, who cooked it for them.

Cuthbert ranged the Northumbrian coast. At a monastery at Tynemouth, monks were floating loads of wood downstream on five rafts. A sudden squall swept them past their landing-place and on towards the open sea. Soon they were so far out that they looked like five birds bobbing on the waves. The brothers on the bank were praying desperately, while across the estuary, a hostile crowd was jeering at their fate. Cuthbert was in the thick of it. He pleaded with them to pray for the monks' safety. The peasants turned on him and told him that the monks were upsetting the old ways so that nobody knew what to do any more. Cuthbert dropped to his knees, bowed his head to the ground and appealed to heaven for help. The wind changed, and the rafts were washed safely back to shore. The story was said to have come from an eye-witness, who said that they all felt shamed by Cuthbert's bearing and had nothing but praise for him after that.

## Cedd

All Northumbria went into mourning for Aidan. King Oswy was repentant. At his wife's insistence, he built an abbey at Gilling on the spot where Oswin had died, and installed a cousin of his wife's as abbot. The king asked for prayers to be offered daily for Oswin's soul and his own. But if Oswy had hoped that with his cousin's death he could become king of all Northumbria, he was disappointed. Oswald's son Oethelwald was now a grown man, and Penda installed him as regent in Deira.

There was more humiliation. Oswy had to hand over his small son Egfrith to Penda's queen as a hostage. Political marriages were arranged. His older son Alchfrith and his daughter Alchfled, children of his British wife Rhiainmelt, were paired with Penda's daughter and son. The marriage of a Christian princess into a heathen kingdom often changed it profoundly. Alchfled's condition for marrying Penda's son Peada was that he be baptized first. Although Penda was one of the fiercest champions of the old English gods, he and his son agreed to this. Peada took instruction from Finan, Aidan's successor on Lindisfarne. As a result, he declared that he would now want to become a Christian regardless of whether he got Alchfled for a wife or not.

Alchfled came to Mercia bringing four Lindisfarne priests with her. Diuma was Irish; the other three were first-generation English Christians, trained in the Celtic tradition. Among these was Cedd, one of those four brothers who had joined Aidan's first intake of schoolboys. Penda allowed them to preach, and they made many converts.

Then Oswy recalled Cedd. He needed a bishop to evangelize Essex, which had remained heathen for 40 years since its brief conversion by the Canterbury mission. Cedd now brought it under the influence of Lindisfarne. King Sigebert was another ruler whose peace-making Celtic Christianity proved too provocative for those barbaric times. Cedd warned him about frequenting the house of a man he had excommunicated – but Sigebert ignored the warning and was murdered there. The reason given by his assassins was that Sigebert was 'too soft on his enemies, and too quick to forgive those who wronged him if they asked for pardon'.

Cedd moved between Essex and Northumbria, founding monasteries in both. His brother Caelin was chaplain to King Oethelwald of Deira. Oethelwald granted Cedd a site for a monastery at Lastingham, on the North Yorkshire moors. Bede describes it as a wild spot, 'fit only for the camps of robbers and the lairs of wild beasts'. In fact, in true Celtic fashion, it was beside a Roman road which led to the court. Cedd embarked on a fast for the 40 days of Lent, to sanctify the site before he started building. Apart from Sundays, he would eat nothing until evening, and then only a small amount of bread, one hen's egg and watered milk. But Cedd had court duties as well. The king called him away before he could complete the fast, so he summoned a third brother, Cynibil, to carry on in his place. The fourth brother, Chad, was away studying in Ireland.

# Wilfrid

Aidan was so deeply loved that, while he was alive, no one brought the difference between Roman and Celtic customs into open conflict. As his successor, Iona sent Finan, another Irishman, whose sister Fina was the princess who had borne Oswy an illegitimate son.

Aebbe, Oswy's sister, asked Finan to make her a nun. She set up her community at a typical site on the cliffs at St Abb's Head and went on to found a bigger abbey at nearby Colding-ham. Like Hild's Hartlepool, hers was a double house.

Finan proved a very different character from Aidan. He was passionately committed to defending Columba's practices and had no patience with those southern Irish churches which had adopted Roman change. Ronan, an Irish scholar from the south, came to Lindisfarne to persuade him. There was a heated argument. Ronan retired hurt.

Listening to their violent encounter was a teenage English boy. Wilfrid was the son of a nobleman. At the age of 14, he left home, finely dressed, with a mounted and armed escort, and presented himself at the Bernician court, bringing letters of recommendation to Queen Eanfled. He wanted her help to enter a life of religion. She was impressed by his good looks and intelligence, but she had a difficulty. She was of the Roman persuasion, but Paulinus had left no abbeys or schools. She did, however, offer an alternative. One of Oswy's warriors, Cudda, was semi-paralysed and had decided to retire to Lindisfarne to become a monk. He would need a personal attendant to look after him. Wilfrid accepted the job. His conduct on Lindisfarne was exemplary. He gained a reputation for devoted service, and filled his spare time with studying in Lindisfarne's library – though he never chose to become a monk there.

His studies fired him with a dream of Rome. Four years later, with Cudda's approval, he appealed again to the queen to help him make this pilgrimage. British and Irish Celts had been globe trotting for centuries, but there was no record of any English pilgrim reaching Rome. Eanfled supplied him handsomely and sent him off to her brother, the king of Kent, but he was made to wait a year in Canterbury for a suitable escort. This proved to be another Bernician, a former warrior in Oswy's service. Bishop Baducing is better known by the name he later adopted in religion – Benedict Biscop.

They stopped in Lyon, where the magnificence of the Gaulish Church made a powerful impression after the poverty of Lindisfarne. Unlike Columban, Wilfrid was not shocked by the riches of ecclesiastical power. Archbishop Annemund ran his palace like a monastery, but ruled the city jointly with his brother, the governor Dalfinus. It was a mixture of private austerity and public splendour. The archbishop became so fond of Wilfrid that he offered to adopt him as his heir. Dalfinus offered his daughter in marriage and part of his territory for Wilfrid to administer. Wilfrid finally tore himself away.

In Rome, Wilfrid singled out as his teacher a man of great influence, the pope's archdeacon Boniface. He learned more about the differences between Roman and Celtic practices, and became passionately convinced of the argument for the Roman case. Then, with the pope's blessing, and gifts of books and relics, he set off back to Britain.

He stopped at Lyon again, for several years, and accepted the monk's tonsure from Annemund. He was still too young to be made a priest. But the Church's politics had antagonized the local queen Baldhild. When Archbishop Annemund and eight bishops were sentenced to death, Wilfrid insisted on mounting the scaffold too. The astonished judges watched him stripping himself for martyrdom and asked who this handsome young man was. When they learned he was English, they told Wilfrid that it was none of his business and packed him off home.

## Whitby

Wilfrid arrived in Britain to find that things had changed dramatically. Oswy had made a reckless bid to free Northumbria from Mercian domination. He vowed to God that if he won, he would give the Church 12 estates and his baby daughter as a nun. Then he led his war-host south. A flash flood swept down on the battlefield, drowning more Mercian warriors than Oswy's soldiers slew. Penda died, still in his battle-armour at nearly 80. With his death, Alchfled's Christian husband Peada became king of southern Mercia. Her Irish chaplain Diuma was installed as bishop, with an abbey at Repton.

It was time for Oswy to make good his oath. Eanfled's one-year-old baby, Aelfled, was taken to Hartlepool and given into Hild's care. Oswy gave the Church 12 small estates. One was Streaneshalch, a site on the cliffs of Deira, known as 'the Bay of the Lighthouse' – now known by its Viking name, Whitby. With the energy for which she was famous, Hild set about building a new monastery there in the Celtic style, with scattered huts, each housing one or two nuns or monks, a school, refectory, guest-house, library. No one church could accommodate all its inhabitants. There were several oratories. There was a house set apart for novices, to which Hild brought the three-year-old princess Aelfled. Above all, Whitby became famous for its school. Hild insisted on a thorough study of the Scriptures. She educated many of the next generation of church leaders. When the ruins of Whitby were excavated, more styluses were found than spindle-whorls.

## Wilfrid and Cuthbert

Wilfrid returned, determined to establish the sort of church he had seen in Lyon and Rome. But he went first to Wessex. After a lapse into heathenism following defeat by Penda, its Church had been put into the hands of a Frankish bishop Agilbert, who followed Roman customs. But he was a poor linguist and King Coenwalh had grown tired of his mutilations of the English language. Coenwalh brought in an Englishman, Wini, from Canterbury, and split Wessex into two dioceses. Agilbert retired to Paris, insulted.

Coenwalh introduced Wilfrid to Alchfrith, Oswy's son and

sub-king of Deira. Alchfrith was ambitious to take his father's place as king over all Northumbria, and he had acquired a reputation for treachery. He and Wilfrid became close friends. Wilfrid won Alchfrith over with his enthusiastic account of the glory of Continental churches. Alchfrith granted him land for a monastery at Stanford, where Wilfrid introduced the Rule of Benedict.

Alchfrith had already given land for an abbey at Ripon and brought in Eata of Melrose as abbot. These monks were Celtic-trained, but they now had English leaders. Eata brought Cuthbert with him as guest-master, and Cuthbert set about the job with his usual energy and dedication. One bitter snowy morning, it is said, he found a young man in the guest-house. Cuthbert gave him water to wash his hands and knelt down to bathe the visitor's feet himself. Finding them almost frozen, he warmed them against his breast and rubbed the circulation back. The young man was eager to be on his way, but Cuthbert begged him to wait until after the midday service, when a meal would be served. He brought some food, and went back to the kitchen to see if the bread had finished baking. When he returned, the visitor was gone, leaving three fine white loaves, smelling deliciously. There were no footprints in the snow.

Converted to Wilfrid's vision, Alchfrith now gave the monks of Ripon an ultimatum: either they adopted the Roman calendar and tonsure or he would throw them out. They refused. Singing a litany of lament, they processed out of the gates, back to Melrose. Alchfrith installed Wilfrid as abbot of Ripon.

Soon after their return, plague struck Melrose. Cuthbert fell sick and the other monks spent the night in prayer for his safety. Next morning, Cuthbert got to hear about it and exclaimed, 'What am I doing lying here? God will certainly answer the prayers of so many good men. Hand me my shoes and staff.' Weak as he was, he got out of bed. He recovered, slowly, but his health was never as robust afterwards.

His friend and teacher, the prior Boisil, did not survive the epidemic. Feeling that he had no more than a week of active life left to him, he called Cuthbert to him. 'You'd better make the most of the time, if you still want to learn from me. By next week, I may be too weak to talk.' 'What book can we get through in a week?' asked the practical Cuthbert. Boisil had a commentary conveniently divided into seven sections. It was on St John's Gospel, the favourite of the Celtic Church. By means of laying aside weighty theological arguments and concentrating on the essence of John's message – the faith which works by love – they just managed it. Cuthbert became prior of Melrose in Boisil's place.

Alchfrith enjoyed Wilfrid's society so much that he wanted him always at court, and never tired of asking him questions. Agilbert, the Frankish bishop who had left Wessex with injured feelings, paid him a visit and Alchfrith begged him to ordain Wilfrid. Wilfrid would not have consented to be priested by a Celtic bishop, doubting the validity of their consecration. But he accepted ordination from Agilbert.

It was Alchfrith who precipitated the Synod of Whitby in 664 (or, as some now think, 663), probably for political as well as ecclesiastical motives. It may have been a move against his father Oswy, who supported the Celtic Church. The synod was originally to be for Deira only, to settle whether the Roman customs of Wilfrid's Ripon or the Celtic style of Hild's Whitby should prevail. The very question shows an important difference. The Celtic party, though resolute in sticking to their own traditions, made few attempts to force others to conform. Wilfrid took another view: all authority was vested in Rome; any departure from it was at least rebellious, at worst heretical.

Hild stood to lose most. It was not just Easter and the tonsure: this decision was about authority. The Roman Church was governed by bishops, the Celtic Churches through their abbots. As abbot of Whitby, Hild had a secure place in the councils of the Church. She taught bishops. She could not be a bishop herself. If the Celtic Church lost, it was the beginning of the end for women like her.

# 14

## *Whitby*

### *The Synod of Whitby*

Hild was to host the decisive gathering at her abbey at Whitby
– Wilfrid's smaller monasteries could not have accommodated
all the delegates. Alchfrith had intended the synod to be for
Deira; it is not clear why Bernicia became involved, since
Oswy and his queen had lived with their differences for
many years. Perhaps Hild appealed to him as paramount
king of Northumbria for help. It was King Oswy, not his
son Alchfrith of Deira, who took the chair.

Oswy was a supporter of Iona's tradition, as was Abbess
Hild. Colman, abbot of Lindisfarne and bishop of Northumbria, led the Celtic side. They also had Cedd, himself an
abbot and bishop, who acted as interpreter, speaking
English, Irish and Latin. The Roman side could only muster
Romanus, still Queen Eanfled's chaplain, James the deacon,
now advanced in years, and Wilfrid. It was natural that the
episcopalian Roman party should wish to be headed by a
bishop, but there was none of their persuasion in Northumbria. They fell back on Agilbert, the Frankish bishop
who had been ejected from Wessex, to lead their delegation,
accompanied by his chaplain Agatho.

Accounts of the synod present it as a single combat, with
Oswy as referee. As well as the date of Easter, there was
much discussion about the tonsure, but we do not have
details. There must have been general debate, but we do not
know what the others said. Wilfrid's biographer reported

that the whole assembly answered the king's question to them 'with one voice'.

Oswy called the synod into session and directed it to seek unity. Then he invited Colman to speak first. The abbot of Lindisfarne comes across as a simple, trusting soul, with absolute faith in St John and Columba, the traditional authorities of the Celtic Churches. He presented his case for the Celtic Easter, founded on the example of the fourth evangelist, the disciple whom Christ loved most dearly. It was a moving appeal to Oswy's childhood on Iona.

Agilbert rose to reply. This must have been the moment the Celtic side were relishing. Agilbert's disastrous attempts at the English language in Wessex were well known. It is unlikely that Oswy could follow fluent Latin, so Cedd would have to interpret.

It was then that the Roman party dropped their bombshell. Agilbert announced that he was handing over as spokesman to Wilfrid.

The whole situation changed. Wilfrid was an Englishman with a sharp mind and a persuasive tongue. He could appeal directly to the king in his own language. Wilfrid claimed his own authority – Rome, city of Peter and Paul. He pointed to the practice of the Church on three continents, all but for a few idiot Scots, Picts and Britons on the uttermost islands in the ocean.

Colman upheld the higher status of St John. Wilfrid rubbished his claim: 'Of course I'm not accusing John of stupidity, but . . .' He pointed out that John had kept Easter on the Jewish Passover, yet the whole Church, including Colman himself, now accepted that it must be a Sunday. Colman quoted an ancient table for forecasting Easter. Then he fell back on his fundamental argument: it was impossible to believe that Columba had been wrong.

Wilfrid tied his audience in knots with a complicated exposition of a different version of Colman's calendar. In fact, Wilfrid himself had an insecure grasp of the complexities, but Colman was not to know that. Far worse was to come. Wilfrid mocked Columba's 'primitive simplicity'. The only possible excuse for him was the isolation of Iona. If Columba had really known what he was saying, he would stand condemned at the Day of Judgement. He might hear his Lord say, 'I never knew you.'

That was an appalling thing to say to the abbot of Lindisfarne. To monks from Iona, Columba was second only to Christ. Colman was incapable of making a rational answer.

Wilfrid contrasted Columba with Peter. He quoted the saying of Christ in Matthew's Gospel: 'You are Peter, and on this rock I will build my Church, and I will give you the keys of the kingdom of heaven.' King Oswy threw this back to Colman: 'Is that really what the Gospel says?' True scholar that he was, Colman could not deny the Scripture. 'And was the same authority given to Columba?' 'No.' Colman was manoeuvred into accepting Wilfrid's inference that Peter's successor in Rome had absolute authority over all issues. Oswy confessed his fear that, if he contradicted Peter, he might be refused admission at the gates of heaven. He gave his judgement for Wilfrid. The Northumbrian Church must conform to the Roman pattern.

It was an incredible reversal of expectations. A king brought up on Iona, giving his verdict against Lindisfarne? Oswy appeared to be giving in to his son and rival, Alchfrith. Why? Oswy's religious fear may well have been genuine. He had murdered Oswin, his kinsman and an anointed king. He had reason to doubt his reception at the bar of heaven. But Wilfrid's biographer says that Oswy pronounced his judgement 'with a smile'. Political undercurrents were at work as well. Alchfrith had made this bid to separate Deira from Bernicia. Oswy could have imposed Iona's rules on the whole of Northumbria, but at the risk of precipitating open rebellion from his son. His decision secured what he had fought for since his accession – a united Northumbria, with himself still firmly in charge. Oswy may have sacrificed Lindisfarne, and all it stood for, to hold on to power. We hear no more of Alchfrith.

# Decisions

The effect on the Celtic camp was consternation. Colman declared that he could not stay on Lindisfarne and accept the changes. Hild stayed loyal to Northumbria: she had not run when Edwin died and she would not leave now. Against her inclination, she instituted the changes at Whitby. Though her name means 'battle', she had the reputation of a woman who counselled peace. Yet she could not bring herself to forgive Wilfrid for the rest of her life.

Colman packed his bags and left for Iona, accompanied by both Irish and English monks. King Oswy took one revenge on Wilfrid. He did not appoint him, or any other Roman supporter, to take Colman's place as abbot of Lindisfarne. He chose Eata, the abbot whom Wilfrid had ousted from Ripon.

The grieving Colman and his loyal monks moved first to Iona and then on to Ireland, to Innisboffin, the 'Isle of the White Heifer', off the Connemara coast. There, unity broke down. The practical English monks complained that the footloose Irish brothers were wandering all over the place in summertime, leaving them to do the work of getting the harvest in. Then when winter came, they expected to come back and be fed. There was a row, and they parted company. Colman found the English monks land of their own on the mainland. The Irish kept the island. It is not recorded how they managed to feed themselves.

Lindisfarne and its daughter abbeys went over to Roman observances. Unlike the tonsure, the underlying spirit of the Church was not so easily changed.

The Synod of Whitby is often referred to as if it decided the issue, ending the Celtic Church – and that this decision affected the whole British Isles. Neither of those things is true. Strictly speaking, there never was a separate Celtic Church. There was not even one single distinctive spirit of Celtic Christianity. The harsh austerity of David's monastery, symbolically closing its gates against newcomers, is very different from the spirit of Brigid, careering across the countryside in her chariot and giving away anything movable to all comers. One truly distinctive Celtic feature was the freedom to differ from what was done elsewhere.

The decision at Whitby has caught the imagination because we have two dramatic accounts of it; the decisions of other kingdoms read more like committee minutes. The Whitby verdict was important, because of Lindisfarne's prestige and Northumbria's ascendancy – but it applied only to Northumbria. The decision to convert to Roman usage had already been taken in some other kingdoms. The south of Ireland went over in the 630s. Comgall's Bangor in the north followed soon after. And other kingdoms held out long after Northumbria had consented. English lands were the easiest targets for the Roman party. The English in Kent had been Roman from their conversion. Essex and Wessex swayed first one way, then the other, with periods of heathenism. Those receiving Christianity from Lindisfarne were now ready to accept Oswy's ruling. Resistance was strongest in the British kingdoms, hostile to the English invaders. For a long time, British Christians would not eat with the English, and scoured any dishes they had used.

Cedd, who won praise for his wisdom as interpreter at Whitby, did not survive long. Plague struck again. Cedd died at his moorland abbey of Lastingham in 664. When his monks in Essex heard the news, they decided to come to Lastingham and die in the same place as their beloved abbot. Only one boy survived. Back in Essex, the result of their reckless self-sacrifice was a return to the worship of Woden for a while. Cedd's brother Chad took over as abbot at Lastingham.

## Change and Continuity

When Colman retreated, heartbroken, from Lindisfarne, Eata moved in. He found the monastery hardly changed since his schooldays. It was still a place of humble poverty. Finan had rebuilt Aidan's leaking church, giving it planked walls and a new thatched roof – but beyond that, there were only the bare necessities for survival. The monks had continued to give away everything they themselves received. They owned nothing of value, save their books, the furnishings of the church and a herd of cows, kept for vellum as well as milk.

Eata invited his prior Cuthbert to join him on Lindisfarne and instil 'a regular discipline'. It was no easy task. The remaining Lindisfarne monks included some who were bitterly opposed to the changes. Insults were hurled at Cuthbert in angry chapter meetings. He remained calm and patient. When tempers became too inflamed, he simply walked out. Next day he returned, quietly insisting on the same requirements, as if nothing had happened. He kept a cheerful face, though it cannot have been easy. He found relief in manual work, and walking around the island asking everyone how they were getting on.

The qualities we most readily associate with Celtic Christianity were very evident in this English saint. His journeys sometimes took him to Coldingham, the double abbey of King Oswy's sister Aebbe. The monks observed that Cuthbert was absent from his cell at night, though he appeared on time for the early morning service. One followed him and saw Cuthbert out in the sea up to his neck, praying, though it was winter. When he came ashore, dripping, shadows flitted across the beach to surround him. Otters were licking his frozen feet to bring the blood back, and wrapping themselves around his body to dry him with their fur.

Cuthbert might have had even more to pray about if he had discovered all that was going on at Coldingham. Aebbe did not rule her abbey with the same regular order as her cousin Hild. Adamnan (not his namesake who later wrote Columba's story) was a Scottish monk there who, in his youth, had committed a sin which he confessed to his soul friend. The penitent Adamnan volunteered to remain standing in prayer all night or to fast for a whole week. The priest counselled something less extreme, so Adamnan settled for eating only on Sundays and Thursdays. His confessor said that he would review the position when he returned from a short absence, but then was suddenly called away to Ireland and died there. Adamnan took the news bravely. Since he had not been

139

absolved, he continued to fast on five days a week for the rest of his life.

Returning from a journey with another monk, Adamnan burst into tears at the sight of Coldingham. Aebbe summoned him to give an explanation. He confessed that a man had appeared to him in the night and told him that he had visited every room in the monastery. His inspection showed a failing institution. Adamnan was the only one devoting himself to a spiritual life. The others, men and women, were either asleep when they should have been praying, or awake and busy with something they ought not to have been. Cells intended for prayer and study were used for eating, drinking, gossip and amusement. The nuns were spending their spare time making themselves attractive dresses. Aebbe reimposed discipline for a while – but after her death things lapsed again. Coldingham burned down in an accidental fire.

## Chad

Wilfrid did not get power in Northumbria as immediately as he might have hoped. Oswy remained in control. He had soothed the Celtic party somewhat by installing Eata on Lindisfarne. But he conformed to the Roman pattern by separating the offices of abbot and bishop, previously held by the same man. From now on, bishops would be more important. The diocese of Northumbria went to Tuda, a southern Irishman used to Roman practice. He died almost immediately. Archbishop Honorius in Canterbury put Wilfrid's name forward as bishop of York.

Wilfrid may have been delighted, but it gave him a problem. In theory, it should not have been difficult to find three neighbouring bishops to consecrate him – or even the preferred number of seven. The trouble was, they would be northern bishops in the Celtic fashion, themselves conse-crated in rites which may have involved only one other bishop. To Wilfrid, their validity was highly dubious – and their attitude to him may hardly have been sympathetic. Wilfrid by-passed Canterbury and went straight to Gaul. He received his episcopal consecration from his friend Agilbert, now bishop of Paris. It was a splendid ceremony. Wilfrid was carried into the sanctuary on a golden chair, surrounded by a throng of bishops. He would have enjoyed that. But he stayed away too long. It may have been that Wilfrid was a man of charismatic presence, whom people could only oppose when he was physically absent. Or Oswy may still have been taking his revenge. Whatever the reason, the king changed his mind, summoned Chad from Lastingham and invited him to become bishop of York.

Chad, raised on Lindisfarne, would have had no personal problem with a consecration by Celtic bishops. But there was a new order now. He was sent to Canterbury for the ceremony. He arrived to find that the archbishop had died – so he went on to Wessex, the see of Bishop Wini from the Canterbury mission. But one bishop was not enough. To assist him at the consecration, Wini enlisted two British bishops. They were probably Cornish, since church relations with the south west were more cordial than with the Welsh. Chad would have seen nothing wrong with that.

He returned to Northumbria and set about travelling his large diocese of Deira, following Aidan's example. He loved to walk the roads, talking to the people he met. Meanwhile a new candidate was sent to Rome to be consecrated archbishop of Canterbury by the pope, but died there before the ceremony could be held. The pope himself selected a man whom he thought suitable for guiding the English Church. Theodore, of Tarsus in Asia Minor, was not in the conventional Roman mode. Before he set out, the pope exacted from him a promise that he would not introduce any dubious Greek customs to his English flock. Theodore even had to wait for his eastern tonsure of St Paul to grow out before his head could be shaved in the Roman way, with the circle of St Peter. He brought with him a store of learning and a new emphasis on church music.

Theodore visited Chad and pronounced his consecration by British bishops invalid. Though the Cornish Church was never expelled from the ecclesiastical family, Theodore was effectively excluding all the non-conforming Celtic clergy from a shared ministry. Chad responded humbly: 'If that's the case, I'll willingly resign. I never thought I was worthy. I only took the job on out of obedience.' Theodore assured him there was no need for that, and reconsecrated him.

The city of York, with its crumbling walls of massive masonry, could not have been to Chad's simple taste, but he fulfilled his commission obediently. When Wilfrid returned from Gaul, there was an almighty row. Oswy ruled that Chad should stay. Wilfrid appealed to Canterbury. Under the new rules, an archbishop in Kent could now intervene in the Northumbrian Church. When he had delivered his verdict at the Synod of Whitby, Oswy had given away some of his own autonomy. Wilfrid was reinstated at York and the humble Chad withdrew to Lastingham, apparently without complaint. When Oswy was asked to provide a new bishop for Mercia, he sent Chad.

Once again, Chad was following in his brother's footsteps. Cedd had gone with princess Alchfled to Mercia when she married. Chad came to Lichfield, and made his hermit's retreat by a well at Stowe, at the other end of the long pool. But Chad, though an Englishman, was even more in the Celtic tradition than his older brother. Cedd rode a horse around Essex. Chad insisted on walking through Mercia. When Theodore came to visit him, he ordered the new bishop to ride a horse on long journeys. Chad begged to be excused. The archbishop lost patience and hoisted Chad into the saddle. Chad does not appear to have followed Aidan so far as to give the horse away to a beggar.

## The Synod of Hertford

In 674, Theodore called together the Synod of Hertford. All the Christian English kingdoms were represented by bishops or their proxies. Kent, Northumbria, East Anglia, Wessex and Mercia all sent delegates. Essex, which had temporarily lapsed into heathenism, and Sussex, which had still not been converted, were not represented. No British kingdoms were invited, and if they had been, some of their church leaders would have refused to meet under the same roof as the English. Hild is listed as one of the main protagonists at the Synod of Whitby. No abbess had a place at the Synod of Hertford. The resolutions of that meeting show how far the character of the Church was changing, for those who had first been brought the Gospel from Iona or from Ireland.

Easter, of course, was to be celebrated according to the Roman calendar. No bishop was to interfere in another's diocese, a bishop was forbidden to interfere with the monasteries. Monks were to stay under a vow of obedience; they were not to wander from one monastery to another, unless they had a letter from their own abbot releasing them. Clergy were not free to leave their bishop and go elsewhere, without a letter of authorization from the bishop, and no one was to receive those who did. No priest was to exercise his calling without permission from the bishop of that diocese. Synods were to be held every year. Bishops were to have seniority through the date of their consecration. More bishops were needed.

The message was clear. Bishops, not abbots, were now in charge. The unit of management was the geographical diocese, not the monastery or the itinerant saint. Stability and obedience to superiors were essential virtues. There was no role at the centre for women. The Celtic vision of the abbeys as inspirational policy-makers, and of pilgrim saints setting out on an open-ended journey to find their place of resurrection, had no place in this new stable order.

## Hild and Caedmon

In the north, the women did not go quietly. When Wilfrid appealed to Rome against his first banishment, the prosecution against him was led by representatives of Abbess Hild and Archbishop Theodore. In his old age, he appealed to the Synod of Nidd to restore him after a second banishment. Abbess Aelfled was not only invited to that synod, but also spoke powerfully in his favour. Wilfrid's biographer speaks of their 'female audacity'.

Hild lived on until 680. That year a remarkable breakthrough was made by a lay man with no scholarship. At this time, God was praised in Latin, or in the Celtic languages. English was a tongue for pagan or profane poetry. In the hall after supper, it was the custom to pass a lyre around, and the one it came to was expected to entertain the company with a song. Caedmon never took his turn. One night, when he saw the lyre coming his way, he escaped from the hall as usual and made his retreat to the byre, where it was his turn to see to the cattle. When he had finished, he lay down to sleep. In dream, a man spoke to him: 'Caedmon, sing me a song.' 'I can't sing. That's why I'm here instead of at supper.' 'You will sing for me.' 'What have I got to sing about?' 'Sing of the creation of the universe.' Caedmon, whose British name suggests that he had Celtic blood in him, began to sing, in English. It was a poem of praise to God, the 'World's Warden', who had raised heaven as a roof-tree. Next morning he awoke, astonished, to find that he could add more verses. He told his foreman, who took him to the abbess and she asked him to sing his song in front of Whitby's best scholars. They recognized a great gift. Since Caedmon could not read Latin, they interpreted a passage of the Scriptures to him and explained its meaning. He returned next morning with another song. Delighted, the abbess invited him to become a monk, and from then on the community fed Caedmon Christian teaching which he transmuted into glorious English poetry. He sang of creation, the Exodus, the Promised Land, Christ's birth, death and resurrection, the Holy Spirit, all the sweep of Christianity to the Last Judgement, in the language of the common people.

For her last six years Hild was in great pain from a burning fever, but she did not give up her vocation of teaching. At 66, she had just founded another monastery at Hackness. In the new dormitory, a nun was awoken by the familiar sound of Hild's handbell, though Whitby was miles away. She opened her eyes to see the roof apparently open and light streaming in as Hild was carried up to heaven. She roused the sisters sleeping around her, and they hurried to the church to pray for Hild's soul. Next morning, brothers arrived from Whitby to tell them that Mother was dead. Whitby passed to Oswy's daughter Aelfled, who had been placed in Hild's care as a baby. For a time she shared the abbacy with her widowed mother, Queen Eanfled. Unlike Hild, they were both supporters of Wilfrid.

## Cuthbert and Egfrith

Oswy was succeeded by his son Egfrith, who soon acquired a reputation for violence. In 672 there was an uprising of Picts on Northumbria's northern border. Egfrith slaughtered huge numbers. The Picts brooded on revenge.

Egfrith next fell out with Wilfrid. First he imprisoned him in an unlit cell, then he banished him. He replaced him with two bishops, one for Deira and one for Bernicia. Abbot Eata was first based at Hexham, but moved his see back to Lindisfarne. Cuthbert was still living there, but he felt ever more strongly the pull to a Celtic hermit's life. Cuthbert retreated to the low black ledges of the Farne Islands in the North Sea opposite Bamburgh – but not for Aidan's temporary fast. He had a cell built of stones with only a hole high up, a 'wind-eye' to God. There was a tiny oratory and a bigger shelter by the landing-place for visitors. He tried to grow wheat in the crannies, and when that failed, barley. For his lavatory, he had a driftwood plank wedged across a gully where the sea washed in and out. Even out on Farne, people flocked to him for advice. His loving monks did their best to look after him, rowing across with food. They took off his boots, which he normally changed only once a year at Easter, and washed his feet. Cuthbert showed them the pig's lard dropped by two penitent ravens. He recommended rubbing their own boots with it to keep them supple. Even so, his shins were stiff with calluses from praying. English though he was, as long as saints like Cuthbert lived, the soul of Celtic Christianity lived on. It was at once immensely attractive and unreasonable.

One of Egfrith's last acts was to force Cuthbert out of obscurity on Farne. Archbishop Theodore came north and decided that Bernicia needed a second bishop. Time and again, messages and letters were sent over to Farne summoning Cuthbert. He would not come. At last, the king and the bishop of York rowed across to fetch him themselves. Cuthbert came in tears. He was appointed bishop of Hexham, but it was so clear to everyone that he would be happier on Lindisfarne that Eata sportingly offered to change places.

The following summer, in 685, the Picts rose again, under a new and more powerful king, Bruide mac-Beli. Cuthbert warned Egfrith not to attack them, but Egfrith ignored him. The Northumbrian war-host was slaughtered at Nechtansmere, her power crippled and Egfrith killed. He was buried on Iona. So, eight years later, was the victor, Bruide mac-Beli. Columba's abbey had been founded in penance for warfare. Now Iona had the power to transcend warring kingdoms.

## Aldfrith

Egfrith was the last of Oswy's legitimate sons. His first queen had refused to consummate the marriage and retired to a monastery. The question of the succession had long been exercising people's minds. His sister Aelfled was abbess of Whitby. The year before the fatal battle of Nechtansmere, she asked for an urgent meeting with Cuthbert, at the monastery of Coquet Island off the Northumbrian coast. She wanted to discuss with him who should become king when Egfrith died. She might be a supporter of Wilfrid, but she still had Hild's ideas about her role in decision making. Cuthbert's reply was enigmatic. He looked round at the islands studding the coastal waters: 'Didn't God make the islands? He's capable of finding us a king on one of them.'

Aelfled knew whom he meant. There remained her halfbrother Oswy's eldest son, born out of wedlock to the Irish princess Fina, sister to Finan who had succeeded Aidan on

Lindisfarne. The Irish called him Flann Fina, 'Blood of the Wine'; his English name was Aldfrith. Since he had not expected to rule Northumbria, Aldfrith's career had been very different from that of the usual English warrior king. He was sent to school on Iona, where his father had once been given sanctuary. But in his case it lit a love of scholarship. He went to Canterbury and on to Malmesbury in Wessex, where an Irish missionary had founded an outpost of Celtic Christianity. Aldfrith travelled extensively in Ireland, studying under the bards, and became an accomplished poet, fluent in Irish, Latin and English.

Cuthbert died two years after his consecration. Feeling his end approaching, he spent his last days on Farne. He asked to be buried there, and had a sarcophagus ready. For five days, the monks who cared for him were prevented from rowing across by a storm. When they arrived, they found that he had hauled himself to the guest-house near the landing stage, to save them trouble. He was lying exhausted. He lifted the blanket and showed them the food he had brought: five onions. One of them was half-nibbled. When death came, a monk waved two torches from the rocks of Farne, and another, looking out from a watchtower on Lindisfarne, ran to the church to report the news of Cuthbert's death to the community. They brought Cuthbert's body for burial, not on Farne, but in the abbey church. Cuthbert was interred with rich Coptic cloth, an ivory comb, a jewelled pectoral cross containing a shell from the Indian Ocean, and his tiny portable altar of oak, embossed with silver.

Cuthbert died an Englishman, obedient to Roman church practices. Yet it is not the tonsure or the date of Easter which characterizes the Celtic Church. At its best, it is a life like Cuthbert's – extreme in personal spirituality, humble service, disregard for comfort, adventurousness, love of wild nature, companionship with women, workers, young people, animals.

Aldfrith turned to another soul friend in the Celtic tradition. Drythelm had been a layman when he had had a near-death experience. Friends and family were already grieving when the body sat up – they all fled in terror, except his wife. He told how he had been to hell and heaven. Hell was a valley flanked by raging fires and bitter winter; heaven, a walled meadow of fragrant flowers. Shaken, he prayed in the village church, then settled his property on his wife, his sons and the poor, and left home. He was summoned to tell his story to Aldfrith, who arranged for him to be admitted to Melrose as a monk. Drythelm was not a man for Benedictine moderation. He could be found up to his neck in the river, praying enthusiastically, even though he had to break the ice first. He refused even to dry his dripping garments afterwards. When the brothers asked how he could bear such cold, he referred briefly to his experience of hell: 'I've known it colder.'

Aldfrith was an eager student and 'a wonderfully wise man'. The seventh abbot of Iona was Adamnan, who wrote Columba's biography, and was himself known as the 'high scholar of the western world'. When a Gaulish bishop was shipwrecked on the west coast of Scotland, Adamnan seized the opportunity to take down his traveller's tales and wrote a comprehensive guidebook to the Holy Land. He made a gift of it to Aldfrith. Adamnan came to Northumbria as an emissary, to arrange the release of hostages taken by Egfrith in a terrible raid on Ireland. The visit had far-reaching consequences. As well as Lindisfarne, Adamnan went to the newer monasteries of Wearmouth and Jarrow, founded by Benedict Biscop, Wilfrid's escort to Lyon. Biscop's Rule was influenced by Continental examples, including the Benedictine. Adamnan was impressed. He returned for a longer visit two years later, and went back to Iona convinced of the case for change. He proposed that Columba's island, and its Dalriadan churches, should adopt the Roman Easter. The community furiously refused. There was no question of Adamnan imposing his will on them. He was more successful in Ireland. At the Synod of Birr in 696, his advocacy was responsible for bringing northern Ireland into conformity with Rome.

He never managed to shift his own abbey. The Britons of Strathclyde went over in 688. Iona finally bowed to change in 716, after Adamnan's death. The Pictish king dropped his resistance and in 718 announced he would expel any rebels who did not change too. The Welsh churches held out until 768, and even then some resisted change. The British kingdom of Dumnonia, in the far south west, had been steadily losing ground before the advance of English Wessex. The remnant in Cornwall was the last Church to keep its Celtic autonomy. It finally came under the authority of Canterbury in 909, more than 200 years after Whitby.

# 15

## *Imagination*

### *Art*

Far from seeing the end of Celtic Christianity, the Synod of Whitby was succeeded by a century which gave us the greatest glory of Celtic Christian art. As the Roman legions had departed, Ninian's students were copying manuscripts to feed the Irish and Welsh libraries, Patrick's embroideresses were beautifying churches, Brigit's craftworkers were painting pictures on Kildare's walls. Those libraries were built up and those churches decorated in a time of barbarian invasion and tribal warfare. Now, Norse raiders came sweeping down with fire and battleaxes. Yet this is when some of the finest treasures of the Christian Celts were created.

There had always been metalwork, for which the Celts were famous. Conlaed, Brigid's bishop, had beautified Kildare's altar with silverware. We can gain a glimpse of what it may have been like from the Ardagh Chalice: a simple silver goblet, banded exquisitely with gold-plated interlace and studded with red enamel and glass bosses. At Nendrum, on Strangford Lough, a workshop was found with pincers and crucibles still containing enamel; there were scraps of slate scratched with trial runs of Celtic designs.

### *Literature*

In the seventh century, when the Celtic–Roman controversy was at its height, there was a flowering of a new type of literature in the Celtic Churches. The *Lives* of Anthony and Martin circulating in Europe led to an outpouring of similar biographies. The *Life of St Samson* was compiled, within 50 years of his death, by a disciple who had worked with Samson and visited places in the story. Jonas's *Life of St Columbanus* was written in around 630, only 15 years after the saint died in Bobbio. There was Cogitosus's *Life of St Brigid*, and the story of the pioneer nun Darerca. Muirchu's *Life of Patrick* and Tirechan's *Memoir* were written to assert the primacy of Armagh against the rival claim of Brigid's Kildare. In contrast to Patrick's own humble writing about himself, they introduced triumphant miracles and made an unsustainable claim that a large number of bishops were created in Patrick's time. In the eighth century, Adamnan, abbot of Iona, wrote Columba's *Life*, using older sources. Bede of Jarrow produced his monumental *History of the English Church and People*, completed in 731. He intended to uphold the Roman cause against Celtic errors, but he is too fair-minded an historian. What shines through his book is the character of the Celtic saints; whereas Wilfrid comes across as insufferable. The *Lives* written in Latin are usually fairly sober accounts. Later ones in the Celtic vernacular become exuberantly imaginative.

There were monastic Rules, liturgical works like the *Antiphonary of Bangor*, and Penitentials. One offered, as a substitute for a year's penance, the 'black fast'. It demanded three days without eating, drinking or sleeping, and three nights, one spent in water, one on stinging nettles, and one on nutshells.

From the eighth century comes the earliest hermit poetry we have. It has created unforgettable images of the woodland retreat:

> A clear pool to wash away sins,
> through the grace of the Holy Spirit,
> facing south for warmth,
> a little stream crossing the clearing . . .
> This is the housekeeping I would get . . .
> fragrant fresh leeks, hens,
> salmon, trout, bees . . .
> and for me to be sitting for a time

praying to God in every place.
(in Jackson, *A Celtic Miscellany*)

Prayer was work. It was necessary to sing prayers for the dead, 'as if every dead believer were a special friend of yours'.

There are attractive images of a scholar, bent over his book at night, looking up to see his white cat, Pangur Ban, crouched at a mousehole.

> I and Pangur Ban my cat,
> 'Tis a like task we are at.
> Hunting mice is his delight,
> Hunting words I sit all night.

That poem, written in Irish, turned up in a library in Austria.

A ninth-century poet imagined Ita, who had given Brendan advice on maritime matters 300 years earlier, acting as wet nurse to the Christ-child: 'Sing a chorus, girls, to the One who has a right to your little tribute; he is in his place on high, though as little Jesus he was on my breast' (in Jackson, *A Celtic Miscellany*). Another, less given to mysticism, confesses that her thoughts wander during the psalms: like a slippery eel, they slide out of her grasp.

There were breastplate hymns, shielding the singer from every assault. We still sing the one that bears Patrick's name, though it was not his composition:

> I bind unto myself today...
> the flashing of the lightning free...
> the whirling wind's tempestuous shocks...
> the stable earth, the deep salt sea

Columba's spirit lived on. We have a poem, perhaps earlier than our twelfth-century copies, imagining his life as a monk on Iona:

> That I might see its splendid flocks of birds, over the
>     full-watered ocean...
> Heaven with its pure host of angels, earth, ebb, flood-tide.
> That I might pore over one of my books, good for my soul;
> a while kneeling for beloved Heaven, a while at psalms.

A while gathering dulse from the rock, a while fishing,
a while giving food to the poor, a while in my cell.
(in Jackson, *A Celtic Miscellany*)

## Books

It should not be supposed that all these books were glories of
Celtic art, illuminated in colour and brushed with gold.
Books were for prayer, for study, for the transmission of
knowledge and ideas. Monks and nuns took them to their
damp cells or read them on a bench outside in the sunlight.
They packed them into leather satchels when they took to
the road or the sea. The great painted works were destined
for the altars of churches, like the one which enthralled those
who saw it at Brigid's Kildare. The most magnificent that
remains is the *Book of Kells*. The title pages glow with the
figures of the evangelists, the winged man for Matthew,
the lion of Mark, the bull for Luke, the eagle of John. There
are carpet pages, covered with interwoven and spiralling
patterns. Hidden in spaces are cats watching mice or kittens,
otters catching fish, a dog seizing a hare. Turn the pages, and
human heads pop out of initial letters, fabulous birds and
beasts contort their bodies in knots, predators prowl along
the line of letters, there are dragons and hens and mermen.
Serpents biting their convoluted tails represent resurrection,
not evil. You can still make out the red dots which guided
the design. They were joined together in a mathematical
sequence to create the knotwork. Turn the page and you see
on the reverse the marks of the ruled lines, the pricks where
the compass points came through. It is possible to detect the
styles of three scribes and at least as many painters.

Each double page of vellum required the skin of a calf. The
*Book of Kells* used at least 150 animals – cattle represented
more than the abbey's milk supply. The blue for the paint
was lapis lazuli from Afghanistan or cheaper woad; red was
supplied by kermes, from insect bodies, or red lead; yellow
came from mineral orpiment; green from verdigris. No gold
was used on the pages of the *Book of Kells*, though the cover

153

was richly decorated with it. The pen was a quill, perhaps from the barnacle goose, to which the eagle of St John sometimes bears a remarkable resemblance. The artist's brush was fine, possibly made of marten fur. Ink was brownish gall or more flamboyant purple, red and carbon black, bound with egg-white or vinegar. The *Book of Kells* was possibly started in the scriptorium of Iona, taken in flight from the Vikings and continued at Kells.

On Lindisfarne, another beautiful volume of Gospels was created by an English monk. It stands in the same artistic tradition, but the Anglo-Saxon influence begins to show: the sinuous curves and spirals are giving way to a more angular interlace.

## Raiders

Eighth-century Europe was an unsafe place, and not just from northern barbarians. In their time, Columban and Gall had overthrown Teutonic sanctuaries in their single-minded fervour. Now, also fervent, also guardians of scholarship, the Moors occupied Spain and invaded France. Columban's Burgundian abbeys were looted and reduced to ruins. The monks and nuns rebuilt.

At the end of the eighth century, Norse raiders attacked the British Isles in force. In Britain, the greatest Celtic abbeys were situated on the coast. In 793, Lindisfarne was raided, its monks stripped and tortured. The English monk Alcuin said that it was a judgement on them for listening to heathen sagas read at dinnertime. In 794 Iona was looted. In 801, longships returned to both islands, killing the remaining monks on Lindisfarne and burning down the abbey on Iona. In 806, the Vikings caught 68 of Iona's monks on the beach and butchered them. Eight years later, most of the survivors packed up what treasures they had managed to hide and moved to Kells in Ireland. They took with them a casket of gold and silver containing Columba's relics. A few remained to rebuild the abbey. In an act of faith, Columba's remains were brought back to Iona and buried in a secret place. In

825, the Norsemen came back, demanding to be told where the casket was hidden. The monks refused to say. There was another massacre.

Ireland's great abbeys were mostly inland. Early casualties were on the coast. Etgal, abbot of Skellig Michael, was carried off to die of hunger and thirst. Bangor was looted. Early in the ninth century the raiders penetrated deeper. The jewels of Ireland's monastic heritage were sacked: Brendan's Clonfert, Ciaran's Clonmacnois, Brigid's Kildare, Finnian's Moville. In Clonmacnois, the Viking queen Audr mounted the altar, from where she led a rite of her gods. In 840 Armagh burned.

Once, scribes had complained in the margins of their books that they could not write properly because of their cold fingers. Now they gave thanks:

> The wind is bitter tonight,
> Tossing the ocean's white hair.
> I need not dread the wild warriors of Norway
> Sailing the Irish Sea.

Wales escaped more lightly, a sign of its poverty at the time.

In 870, the Vikings attacked Aebbe's double house of Coldingham, now an all-women abbey. The nuns mutilated their faces, in the hope that this would spare them rape. The Vikings burned them to death. Five years later, the Lindisfarne brothers abandoned hope of continuing on their low, sandy island. They dug up Cuthbert's remains, and some of Aidan's. Then, with their lay farm workers, they drove their cattle across the sand spit at low tide, and sought a greater safety inland.

These are only the tragedies of the abbeys whose histories we know. Countless isolated hermitages and small communities of monks and nuns went down into oblivion, along with Christian laity. A treasure of people was slaughtered or driven abroad. We can only guess at the art treasures we might have had from those few precious examples which remain. Some of them came heart-stoppingly close to destruction by other means. The *Book of Kells* was stolen from the church. After nearly three months, it was found buried under a turf, with the gold ripped off its covers.

## Sculpture

What the Vikings could not easily loot or destroy were stone crosses. These had wooden forerunners, set up at preaching centres out of doors – but eighth-century artists began to carve them in stone. They stand tall, sometimes as much as five metres high. The equal arms reach out beyond the cosmic wheel. The earliest Celtic crosses did not bear the figure of Christ. Now he appears crucified, between soldiers bearing sponge and lance or, more typically, still on the cross but robed in glory, or as judge. The shaft is alive with scenes from the Bible or Christian legend, set within bands of interlace. The meeting between the desert hermits Anthony and Paul was a favourite subject. Before the spread of stained-glass windows, these outdoor crosses were visual aids to devotion for the common people.

## Pilgrim Scholars

The Celtic spirit proved as durable as the crosses. The Irish were irrepressible. Franks poured into the Irish schools as students; the Irish went to mainland Europe as teachers. They brought knowledge in their heads and books in their luggage. Some of the finest Celtic manuscripts were saved from the Vikings to find a home on the shelves of mainland European libraries. Irish scholars were famous for being the only people in Western Europe to retain the knowledge of Greek. The claim may be exaggerated, but some Irish did have a nodding acquaintance with the language, and a few of them were expert in it. So high was their reputation in continental Europe that the word 'Irish' became equated with 'scholar'.

There were frequent complaints about these immigrants. They were 'too noisy', 'too great a drain on welfare funds', and there were 'just too many of them'. Two Irishmen,

Clement and Albinus, arrived in Aix-la-Chapelle around 791, travelling with a party of British salesmen. They set up their pitch in the market place, calling out, 'If you want wisdom, we're selling.' Charlemagne sent for them and gave them jobs on his staff. As well as expounding the Scriptures, they taught the classical curriculum of grammar, rhetoric, dialectic, arithmetic, including fractions, astronomy, geometry and music. To this they sometimes added medicine, astrology and mechanics. They were as adventurous in their thinking as in their travels. Clement queried Christ's descent into hell. Feargall, or Vergil, was in trouble for writing of another world beneath ours, possibly the Antipodes. Dicuil wrote the first major geography textbook since classical times. He gathered information ranging from accurate observations about the pyramids of Egypt to facts about Iceland which he had gathered from Irish monks who lived there. He assures us that they could pick the lice out of their shirts by the light of the midnight sun. He was not a man to accept popular beliefs without subjecting them to scrutiny: there was an urban myth that elephants slept on their feet, leaning against a tree; Dicuil was able to observe that Abulabat, the elephant given by Haroun-el-Raschid to Charlemagne, slept lying down.

In the ninth century it was said that 'pretty well the whole of Ireland is risking sea travel and migrating to our shores, bringing a herd of intellectuals'. Charles the Bald was the patron of many of them. His most famous protégé was John Scotus Erigena, 'John the Scot from Ireland'. In 845, Erigena was invited to write about Augustine of Hippo's doctrine of predestination, which Pelagius had refuted. Erigena's book went far further than it was meant to: he rejected the objective existence of evil itself; the Garden of Eden was an allegory; evil was the separation of humanity from God. His work was condemned, but Charles protected Erigena. In an even more original work, *On the Division of Nature*, Erigena wrote that the Creator is in everything created, so humans have potential access to all wisdom. Only sin separates us from the divine within us. His mastery of Greek allowed him to inherit the liberal tradition of classical philosophers lost to most of Europe. The story is told that his infuriated students stabbed him to death with their pens. Others say that he went to Glastonbury.

Charles the Bald seems to have taken a more tolerant attitude. There is a famous joke that the king, sitting across the table from Erigena, asked him, 'What's the difference between a Scot and a sot?' Quick as a flash came back the answer. 'Just the table.' Erigena's prayer was that he might use reason to understand the words of Jesus 'without any error or false theory'.

The spirit of Celtic pilgrimage was still alive in 891. King Alfred of Wessex was intrigued to hear that three Irishmen had landed in Cornwall, having set out in a coracle without oars. They said they did not care where they came ashore as long as 'for the love of God, they could be in foreign lands'. Eleventh-century Irish monks, though Benedictine in their Rule, founded a chain of *Schottenklösters*, 'Scots' Cloisters', from Vienna to Kiev.

## The Celi-de

The century after Whitby saw a revival of the hermit ideal. Mael-ruain was abbot of Tallaght, near Dublin. He condemned the prevailing laxity he saw around him and chose the rigorous life of an anchorite, but within reach of a larger community. From his inspiration grew the Celi-de, or Culdees. The name means 'God's Serf', one who is more than a slave, but with a lifelong obligation to work the land of the Lord. It became a movement offering opportunities for monastic and secular, ordained and laity, men and women. Culdees practised an ascetic discipline and had a particular care for education and the disadvantaged. It was said that the Irish saint Moling had a vision of a distinguished young man dressed in purple, who announced himself as Christ, the Son of God. 'That's impossible,' said Moling. 'When Christ comes to talk to the Celi-de, he doesn't come wearing purple, but in the shape of the wretched, the sick and the lepers.'

The movement spread across the British Isles. Macbeth and his wife Gruoch gave land to the hermits on Lochleven. At first, 'Culdee' was almost synonymous with 'hermit'; as the centuries went by, it was more often used to mean irregularity. An orderly hierarchical Church did not know what to do with them. The Culdees must conform or go. In the twelfth century, Malcolm of Scotland's reforming English queen Margaret set about establishing uniformity. She suppressed a 'barbarous ritual', which probably meant a surviving Celtic Gallican liturgy.

The spirit of Celtic Christianity was essentially one of diversity – from the huge abbey-college of Bangor-ys-Coed to a few huts perched on the tip of Skellig Michael out in the Atlantic; from warrior kings like Oswald, translating Aidan's first sermons to his troops, to a hermit woman coming ashore from her coracle in Cornwall; from Penitentials which demanded sleeping on a bed of nettles to those who warned how the Devil had tried to tempt Anthony to excessive fasting. One by one, Churches in the Celtic lands changed their Easter computation, and monks grew their hair in a different fashion. The moderate Benedictine Rule replaced more extreme monastic lifestyles. Emphasis shifted to bishops and the diocesan Church. That did not extinguish overnight Celtic Christianity's enthusiastic creativity, its capacity to imagine new possibilities, its pilgrim spirit, its sometimes reckless abandonment of self for love of God and the disadvantaged.

Their irrepressible spirit challenges us to meet defeat with creativity and adventurousness.

# 16

## *Vision*

It is hard to know where to stop. Some see the Reformation as a continuation of Celtic Christianity's independent thought. Others find links with the Orthodox Churches guarding ancient tradition. Welsh and Cornish non-conformity have that closeness with the common people. The nineteenth century saw Alexander Carmichael tramping the highlands and islands of Scotland to collect the prayers of Gaelic speakers with their threefold blessings, their hallowing of common actions, their memories of Brigid and Columba. Writers today are resurrecting the poetry of Celtic prayer, inviting us to write our own hallowing of modern life. Twentieth-century feminism has claimed it, and the ecology movement. There is a wave of nostalgia sweeping across Britain for a perceived golden age. It has brought us a flood of Celtic Christian books and artefacts.

There was no golden age. Women reached a high point in Irish Brigid's generation, and again in English Hild's; they get little mention in Wales, and many stories denigrate women. We hear hardly anything about lay Christians outside an abbey or hermitage. And democrats would surely prefer the Benedictine choice of an abbot by merit, rather than the Celtic practice of hereditary, usually aristocratic, succession. John Scotus Erigena insisted that we use our heads.

There was no single Celtic Church, and those Churches we call Celtic were flawed. Yet they stir our imagination powerfully. They hold a part of our sacred tradition that we must not lose. Strands interweave through the knotwork. Suddenly, an amazing face pops out of the pattern, and we see it again here, and there. Celtic Christianity celebrates both continuity and creative imagination. For all its faults, it did offer possibilities for women, reverence for God's gift of creation, the vision of taking risks and travelling out in a spiritual quest. There was delight in poetry and scholarship. Celtic Christianity was conservative about rites and customs, but it was also more innovative that it realized. The hermit tradition is essentially subversive of hierarchical authority. It acts on belief in a God who speaks directly to the individual.

Even the Celtic way of dealing with dragons is revealing. St George and St Michael are shown brandishing swords and triumphantly crushing the dragon's head under a mailed foot. Celtic saints use a different technique: Samson tied a stole round the serpent's head, led it away from confrontation and told it to behave itself; Petroc healed the bitterness by taking a splinter out of the dragon's eye.

It would be perverse to claim that these qualities are unique to Celtic Christianity. The mind flies to Francis of Assisi, lover of creation, of poverty and penance. It is illuminating that, early in the thirteenth century, Francis spent time at Bobbio, Columban's last monastery. His own settlements show traces of this Irish pattern, even using the Irish word *carcair* for a cave hermitage, like the one Columban borrowed from the bear.

Celtic saints were rooted in the physical world. Visiting ancient holy places is not the Celtic vision of pilgrimage, but it is still worth doing. Stand at Clonmacnois, Ciaran's great monastic complex on a bend of the river Shannon: imagine a shipload of foreign students coming up the river. Make a journey into the Welsh hills, to where the road runs out at Pennant Melangell, and find in the meadows the ancient church of the girl who protected a hare from the hunter, now a healing centre. Share the weekly pilgrimage round Iona: at the bay where Columba landed, pick up a pebble of your past, cast it into the sea and turn your back on it. Take the pilgrim way to Lindisfarne: abandon the causeway and walk out in faith across the wide wet sands, with one eye for the rising tide and one on your destination.

This century, we are beginning to shake off cultural colonization by Rome and realize that we have our own indigenous tradition. We have discovered that our history is written in Welsh and Irish, as well as in Latin and English. When the Roman legions left, British stubbornness and then Irish imagination created the Celtic Churches to meet a new situation. To honour our Celtic past truly, we must work out, as they did, what it means to be the Church in the British Isles for our own time.

# Further Reading

Adamnan, *Life of Saint Columba*, ed. W. Reeves. Llanerch 1988.

Ailred and Joceline, *Two Celtic Saints: The Lives of Ninian and Kentigern*. Llanerch 1989.

Anderson, M., *St Ninian, Light of the Celtic North*. Faith 1964.

Backhouse, J., *The Lindisfarne Gospels*. Phaidon 1981.

Baring-Gould, S. and Fisher, J., *Lives of the British Saints*, ed. D. Bryce. Llanerch 1990.

Baring-Gould, S., *Lives of the Northumbrian Saints*. Llanerch 1990.

Bede, *A History of the English Church and People*. Penguin 1968.

Bradley, I., *The Celtic Way*. Darton, Longman and Todd 1993.

Bradley, I., *Columba: Pilgrim and Penitent*. Wild Goose 1996.

Chadwick, N. K., *The Age of the Saints in the Early Celtic Church*. Llanerch 1960.

Chadwick, N. K., *The Celts*. Penguin 1970.

Doble, G. H., *The Saints of Cornwall*, ed. D. Atwater. Dean and Chapter, Truro 1960.

Farmer, D. H. (ed.), *The Age of Bede*. Penguin 1983.

Flower, Robin, *Poems and Translations*. Lilliput Press 1994.

Hanson, R. P. C., *The Life and Writings of the Historical Saint Patrick*. Seabury 1987.

Henig, M., *Religion in Roman Britain*. Batsford 1984.

Henry, F. (ed.), *The Book of Kells*. Thames and Hudson 1974.

Hood, A. B. E. (ed.), *St Patrick: His Writings and Muirchu's Life*. Phillimore 1978.

Jackson, K. H., *A Celtic Miscellany*. Penguin 1971.

Jackson, K. H., *Studies in Early Celtic Nature Poetry*. Llanerch 1995.

Leatham, D., *Celtic Sunrise*. Hodder and Stoughton 1951.

Lehane, B., *Early Celtic Christianity*. Constable 1994.

McNeill, J., *The Celtic Churches: a History AD 200 to 1200*. University of Chicago 1974.

Marsden, J., *Northanhymbre Saga*. Kyle Cathie 1992.

Mayr-Harting, H., *The Coming of Christianity to Anglo-Saxon England*. Batsford 1972.

Metlake, G., *Life and Writings of St Columbanus*. Llanerch 1993.

Morris, J., *The Age of Arthur*. Phillimore 1977.

Ordnance Survey, *Map of Britain in the Dark Ages*. Ordnance Survey 1974.

Rees, B. R., *Pelagius: A Reluctant Heretic*. Boydell 1988.

Reeves, W., *The Culdees of the British Isles*. Llanerch 1994.

Ross, A., *Pagan Celtic Britain*. Constable 1992.

Severin, T. *The Brendan Voyage*. Hutchinson 1978.

Stokes, W. (tr.), *The Lives of the Saints from the Books of Lismore*. Llanerch 1995.

Taylor, T., *The Life of St Samson of Dol*. Llanerch 1991.

Thomas, C., *Christianity in Roman Britain to AD 500*. Batsford 1985.

Thompson, E. A., *Saint Germanus of Auxerre and the End of Roman Britain*. Boydell 1984.

Toulson, Shirley, *The Celtic Year*. Element 1993.

Winterbottom, M. (ed.), *The Ruin of Britain and other works*. Phillimore 1978.

# Index and Glossary

167